# CONSTRUCTING RADIANCE

## Sculpture by Li Hongwei

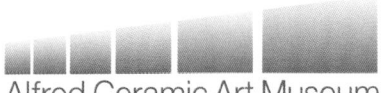

Alfred Ceramic Art Museum

September 26, 2024 – March 30, 2025

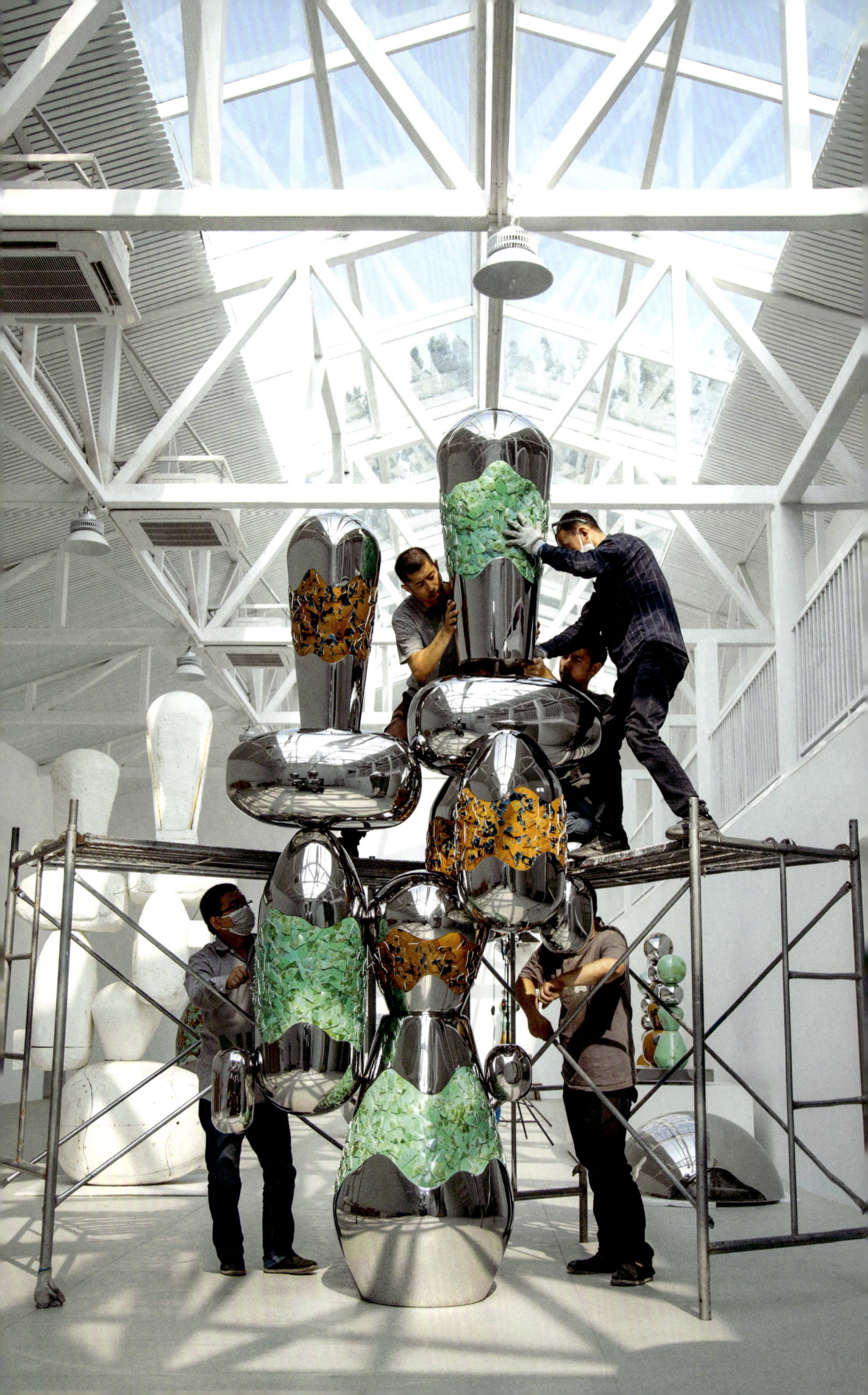

# CONTENTS

7

LOOKING BACK: A WINDOW ON THE PRESENT
Wayne Higby

21

MATERIALS, MINDFULNESS, MASTERY:
THE ART OF LI HONGWEI
Denise Patry Leidy

33

THE PHENOMENOLOGY OF GRAVITY IN THE WORK
OF LI HONGWEI
Benjamin Evans

42

GALLERY
Photography by Brian Oglesbee

70

LI HONGWEI SELECTED RESUME

72

WRITERS' BIOGRAPHIES

74

EXHIBITION CHECK LIST

76

COPYRIGHT PAGE

WE CANNOT
CONTROL THE
LENGTH OF LIFE,
BUT WE CAN
CONTROL ITS
HEIGHT.

-LI HONGWEI

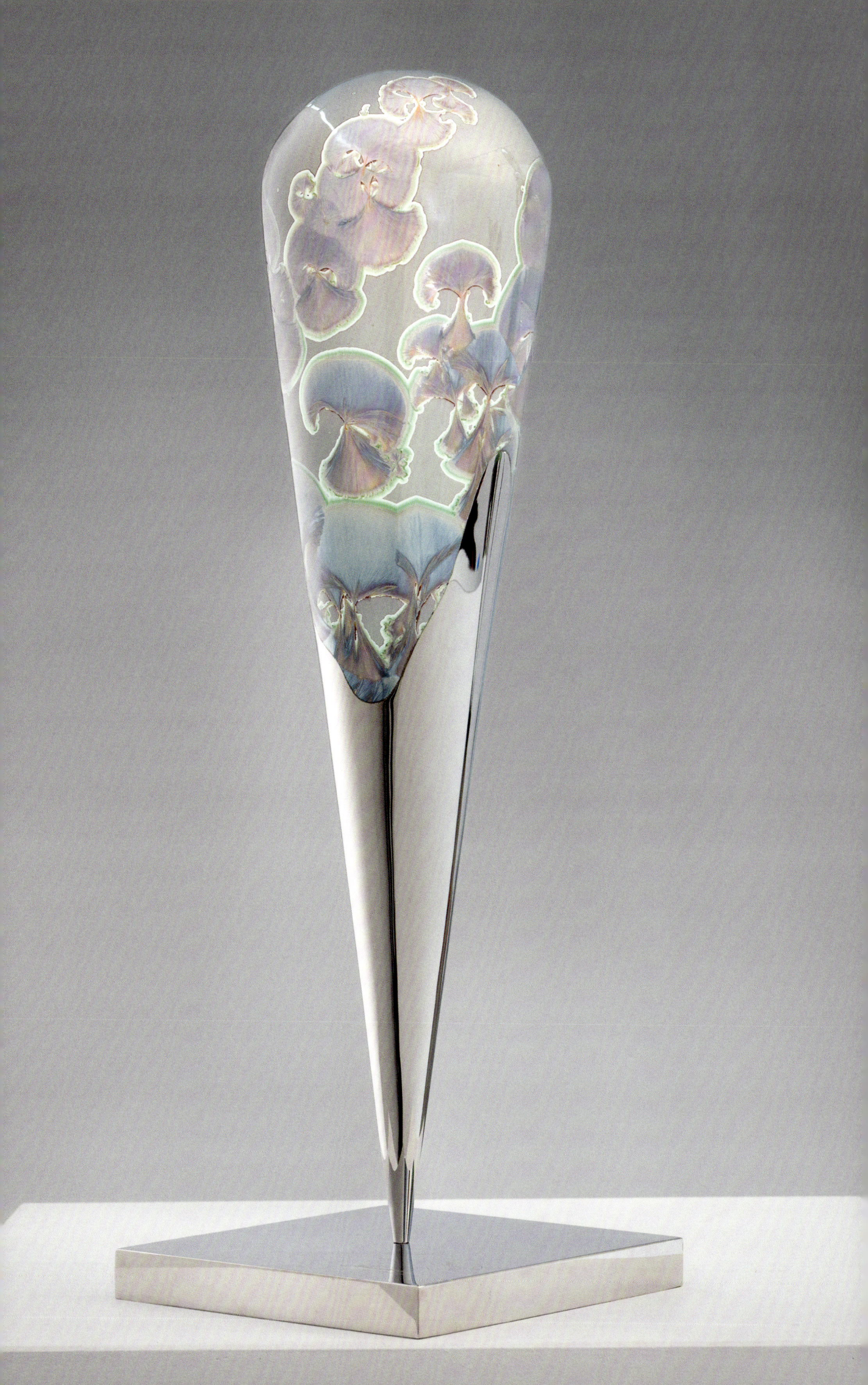

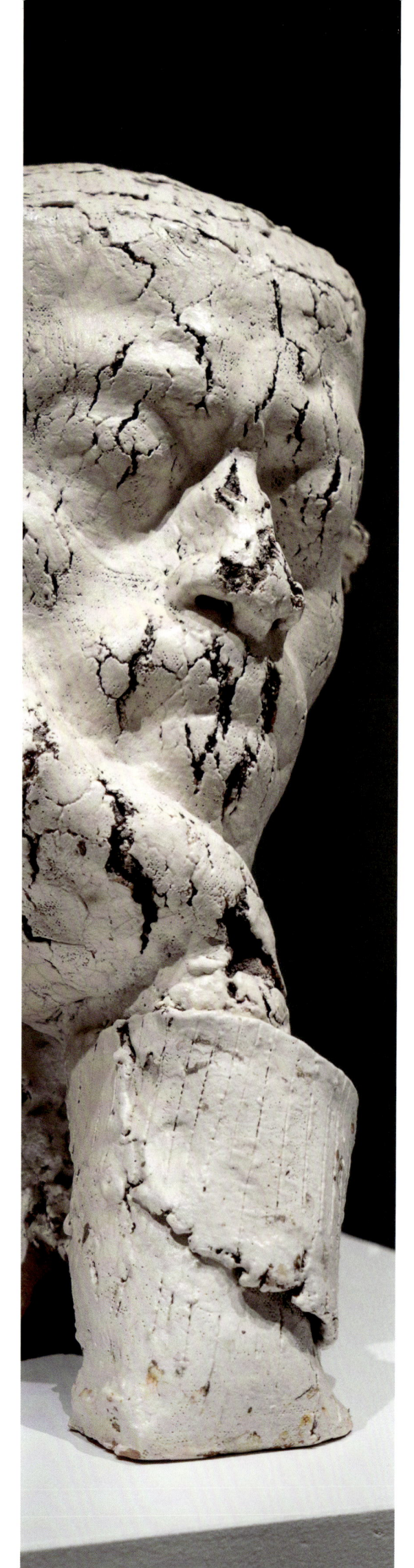

# LOOKING BACK: A WINDOW ON THE PRESENT

WAYNE HIGBY

*Constructing Radiance: Sculpture by Li Hongwei* was chosen as an exhibition title early on in the development of the Alfred Ceramic Art Museum's presentation of Li Hongwei's art. I wrote a short piece of wall text to illuminate the title:

> Sculpture, a product of constructing forms in three-dimensional space, is embedded in the history of human endeavor and is often associated with a search for meaning. Radiance is an ephemeral condition, a reflection of light or a rare luminosity. Radiance often suggests an exquisite harmony as universals underlying reality unite in timeless balance. These words which contextualize the current exhibition suggest a framework for contemplating the ever-expanding achievement of sculptor Li Hongwei.

Li was born in Tangshan, China. As a youth he exhibited interests in calligraphy, painting, mathematics and athletics. Li passed the highly competitive entrance exam for admission to the prestigious Central Academy of Fine Arts, Beijing. There he received formal training in sculpture, graduating with a BFA in 2005.

*Li Hongwei,* Power of Silence*, 2006, earthenware, 18 x 14 x 12 inches.*

That year I became a witness to Li Hongwei's remarkable journey as an artist. Anticipating his graduation from the Central Academy of Fine Arts, Li applied to be a candidate for the Master of Fine Arts degree in ceramic art at the New York State College of Ceramics, School of Art and Design at Alfred University, Alfred, NY. As a professor of ceramic art I was on the committee that chose eight candidates for the degree from approximately 100 applicants. Li was one of the eight who arrived at Alfred in the fall of 2005. By then I had already met him.

Earlier that summer I was doing a workshop in Beijing at the Central Academy of Fine Arts. On Monday May 23, 2005, Li Hongwei came to the workshop and introduced himself to me. "I am coming to Alfred," he said. I responded, "Yes, I know." He wrote his name in English and Chinese in my journal and left his phone number. On Friday May 27 we had dinner together. That was the beginning of a long and extraordinary professional relationship.

The following is an excerpt from: *Cultivating Dualities: A Conversation with Li Hongwei* which was a question-and-answer session facilitated by Michael Amy for Sculpture Magazine, 5/22/2019.

> Li Hongwei:  The Department of Sculpture at the Central Academy of Fine Arts (CAFA) in Beijing has a "five-year program that borrows its educational approach from the École des Beaux-Arts in Paris and the Repin Institute of Arts in St. Petersburg. Students in the sculpture department were trained to create realistic renderings of the human body. Our styles back then were inspired by the works of Michelangelo, Carpeaux, and Rodin. During my five years at CAFA, I worked hard to improve my technical skills and my understanding of space. I have come to appreciate the rigorous training that I received there. I also looked at other approaches and produced some abstract sculpture during those years, working with steel, bronze, and different types of clay.

Li Hongwei includes the following comment in his conversation with Michael Amy:

> For me, clay has a special power in the way that it takes on shape and changes. It is capable of seizing my emotions, movements, and memories. Back then, I could not feel anything close to a comparable connection with other materials, and I spent my last two years at CAFA experimenting with fired clay. I love the feeling of clay—this is why I went on to study at Alfred.[1]

In contrast to Li Hongwei's undergraduate background, the pedagogical approach regarding the MFA program in ceramic art at Alfred University begins with the assumption of a fundamental ceramic material and process skillset as a baseline determined via the application process. The primary emphasis of the program is based on expanding those skills with a focus on the individual artist as maker. Following, informing and supporting the individual artist's intuition and initiative is a primary goal of the program. The study of art history, particularly ceramic art history across a wide spectrum as well as ceramic materials course work, seminars and highly intensive studio work are required within the frame of faculty-student interactions.

At Alfred, in the fall of 2005, I was assigned to be Li Hongwei's graduate advisor and to work with him through out his first semester. He had been drawing some self-portraits in his sketch book. So that was a place to begin. As it worked out, I was also his advisor for his final thesis semester. Later I wrote an essay "Self-Portrait: The Art of Li Hongwei" for the first book on his work, *Beyond Reflection: The Art of Li Hongwei* published by Pucker Art Publications in 2018. That text began with the following paragraph:

> Li Hongwei is among the new generation of artists who have taken a deeply rooted, Chinese national identity and revolutionized it via individual perspectives. His achievement in ceramic art is especially significant. Li Hongwei's acceptance into the renowned Master of Fine Arts program in ceramic art at Alfred University marked a significant step in his development as an artist and a significant step in the arc of his life. For Li Hongwei, studying in America brought his personal life story into deep scrutiny. The cultural diversity between China and America offered a comparative analysis that focused the challenging question: Who am I? In an attempt to answer that question, the artist began a series of self-portraits in fired clay.[2]

Li's cross-cultural educational experience established a foundation for his art as he fused both classic Chinese cultural history with attention to Western philosophical discourse established in the history of Modernism and contemporary art. Li's combination of East and West cultural immersion, along with a sophisticated investigation into ceramic technique, has led to his international recognition as an important sculptor of our time.

Li graduated in 2007 and remained in Alfred teaching freshman in the foundations program of the Art and Design School. In the spring of 2008 he called me and asked if we could have a conversation. During that conversation he said that he planned to return to China and we began to brainstorm what he might do there to earn a living.

In 2008, I was in the process of working on an architectural project now entitled *EarthCloud* commissioned by Alfred University alumnus Marlin Miller for a performing arts complex he was building for the University. At that time, Miller offered me an additional architectural commission for a theater that he was also building in Reading, Pennsylvania. I began to consider the Reading project as something I could facilitate in collaboration with a factory in China. But how?

W. Higby China Journal entry 6/4/2008: Individuality Art Ceramics factory, Foshan China.

> Li Hongwei is here. Hongwei just graduated from Alfred with his MFA. He is one of the important reasons to try to do this project now. The plan is for him to move to Foshan, get a studio, a place to live and oversee the project at the factory until it is finished.

Foshan, translated as "Buddha's Mountain," is one of the largest ceramic tile production centers in the world. Li Hongwei lived in Foshan for a year from the summer of 2008 to fall of 2009. He was able to establish a studio for his own work at the Nanfeng Ancient Kiln cultural site in Foshan. Li produced a new series of self portrait heads based on a monumental piece he made for his graduate thesis exhibition. (Fig. 1 + 2)

During this period I made 5 trips to the factory and at other times consulted directly with Li by email and phone from my Alfred studio. From the onset of the project Li demonstrated a charismatic way of translating my vision as he explained the details of my thinking on how together we could make something beyond our previous experience. His exceptional bilingual skill at the factory helped immeasurably from the first day to create an atmosphere of friendship and commitment to an unknown artist from America. Perhaps growing up in Tangshan, a major industrial city referred to as the "porcelain capital of North China," gave Li a special intuitive insight into the soul of a mega factory city and its hard-working population. (Fig. 3)

This introduction to the artist Li Hongwei and his exhibition at the Alfred Ceramic Art Museum is intended as a biographical sketch of the artist which attempts to offer insight as to the background story behind the art itself. As such it is interesting to note that not only is Tangshan, China, the northern capital of porcelain manufacture, it is also the world's largest steel producing center. It would be misguided to draw any direct relationship between Li's art in steel and porcelain. However, early years immersed in the life of an industrial city empowered by a work force of makers might lead to a subconscious acquisition of knowledge and to the eventual discovery that tireless work with ancient and modern materials would be for Li his characteristic signature as an artist. This lends a bit of context to the discourse about Li Hongwei's art which includes speculation on the cultural differences of East and West as well as the history of media.

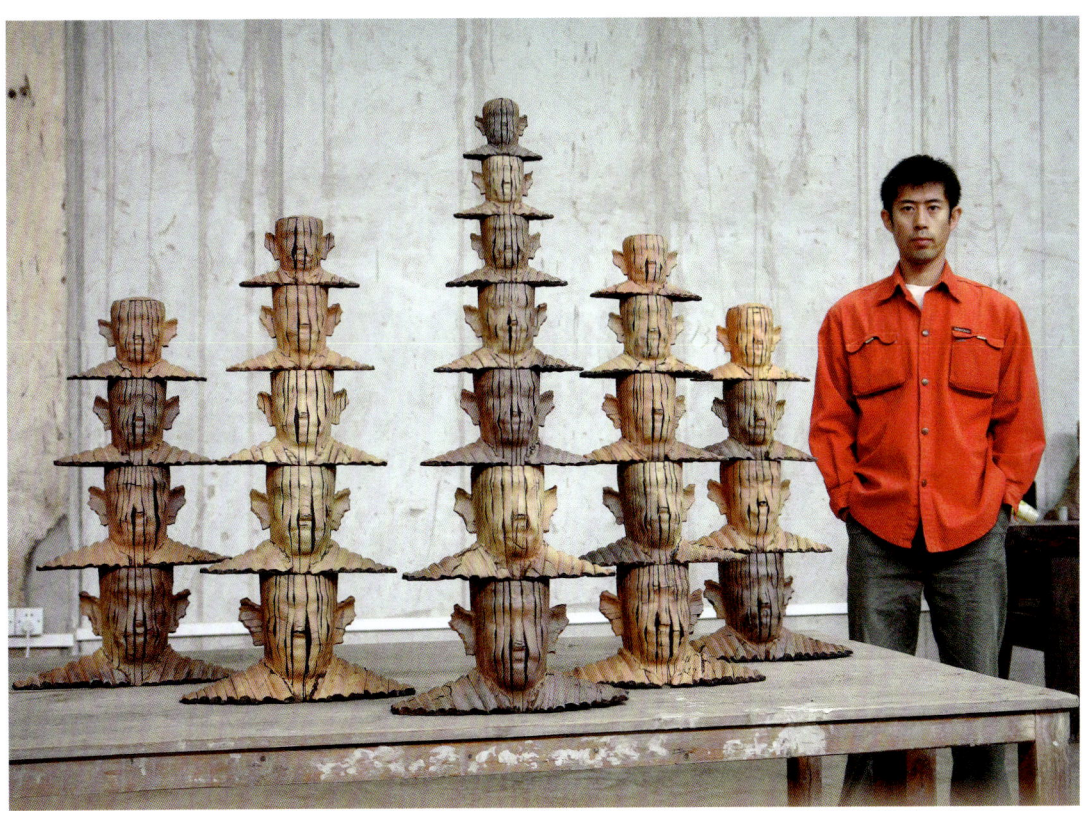

Fig. 1: Hongwei, first studio post grad school, Foshan, China. Photo Li Hongwei archive

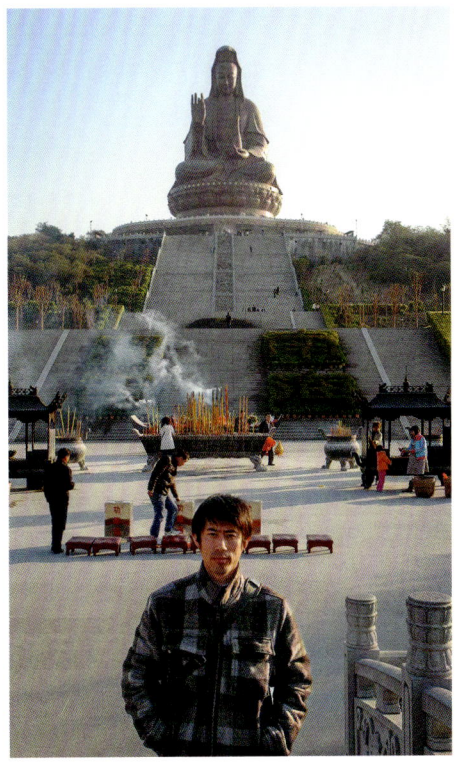

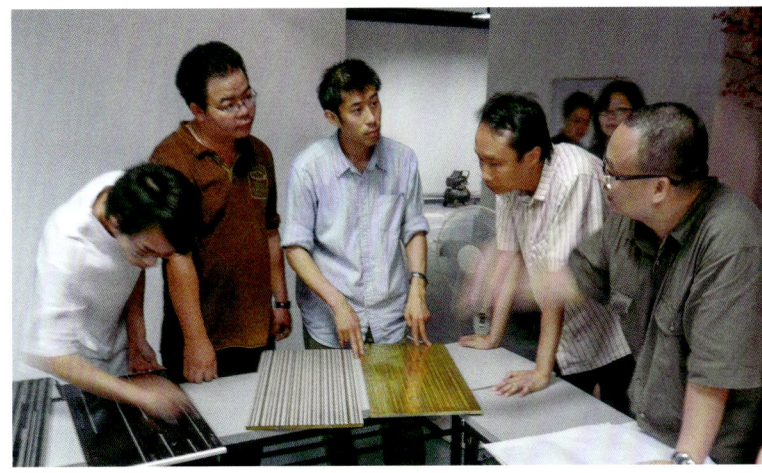

Left: Fig. 2: Li Hongwei at the Guanyin Temple on Mount Xiqiao, Foshan, China. Photo Higby archive

Above: Fig. 3: First day at the factory with Li Hongwei, Foshan, China. Photo Higby archive

With Li's continued help, the Reading project, renamed *SkyWell Falls*, was installed at the Miller Center for the Arts, Reading, Pennsylvania in the fall of 2009. Once the installation was completed Hongwei returned to China.

W. Higby China Journal entry 6/4/2010: Tangshan, China.

> Long awaited trip to Tangshan to visit Li Hongwei's home town. We have often talked about a trip to Tangshan which is about 2 1/2 hours NE of Beijing.

Li Hongwei and I spent the day touring Tangshan which included lunch with his parents and a visit to their home where Li grew up. One particular topic on that day of reminiscing about Li's youth included a conversation about drawing. The following is a quote from Li Hongwei's graduate MFA Thesis Report required as part of the thesis exhibition held at the conclusion of the two years of graduate study.

> When I was a child, I liked drawing architectural designs, but mostly, I drew our house over and over. When I moved later to go to school in Beijing and now in Alfred, I always keep the memory of the physical places where I lived foremost in my memory - places that signify home, safety, warmth. I've never stopped drawing the places where I live, each one different in its own way. [3]

Li Hongwei's propensity for drawing took on increased dimension as a student at the Central Academy of Fine Arts where observational drawing serves as a fundamental exercise in skill development. The ability to concentrate and render objectively the human figure or still life requires a discipline seldom acquired by contemporary American art school students. Drawing is the most direct, immediate access to the artist's eye, hand and mind. Often it signals an emotional intelligence as well as a tracking of the interface between an artist thinking and the world at large. It can serve as a planning device, a first stage problem solver or a record of a feeling in pictorial form. Li's foundation as a disciplined observer was there since childhood and grew exponentially as a mature artist. Today we see this in the intense attention to detail incorporated into each element of his sculpture. The fluidity embedded in the interchange of parts to the whole as well as the unity and balance that give the work its powerful presence are at its core a possibility of imagination tied to a life of observation and drawing as exploration. (Fig. 4)

Numerous trips in China with Li Hongwei included visits to five different studios as his career began to develop. As I have mentioned, his first studio was in Foshan during the making of *SkyWell Falls*. His second studio was a small one, as might be expected in Beijing, but the work continued to reveal an intensity that was a clear signal of exceptional

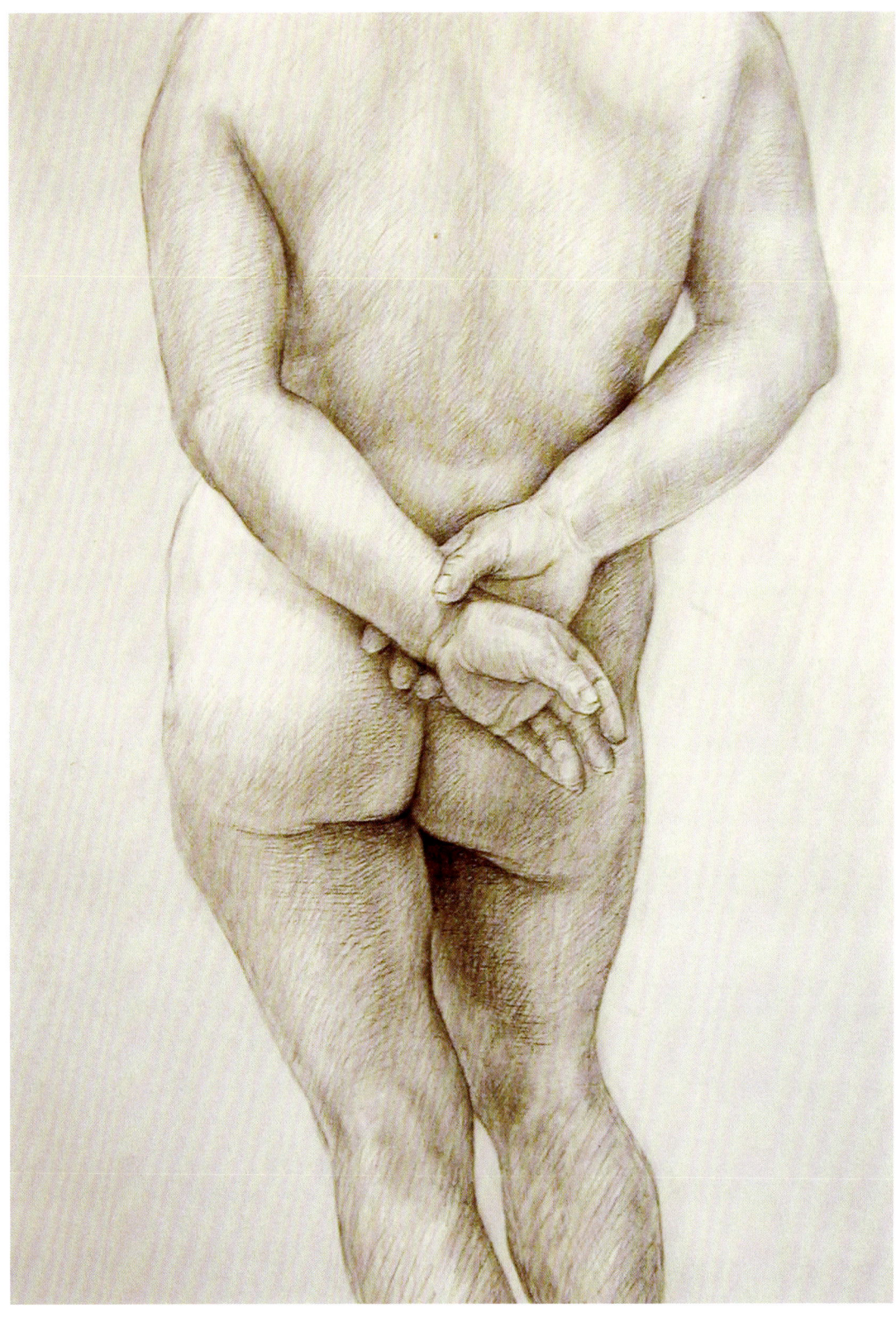

*Fig. 4: Li Hongwei, Life Model Drawing, 2001, pencil on paper 31 x 43 inches.*
*Photo Li Hongwei studio, Beijing, China*

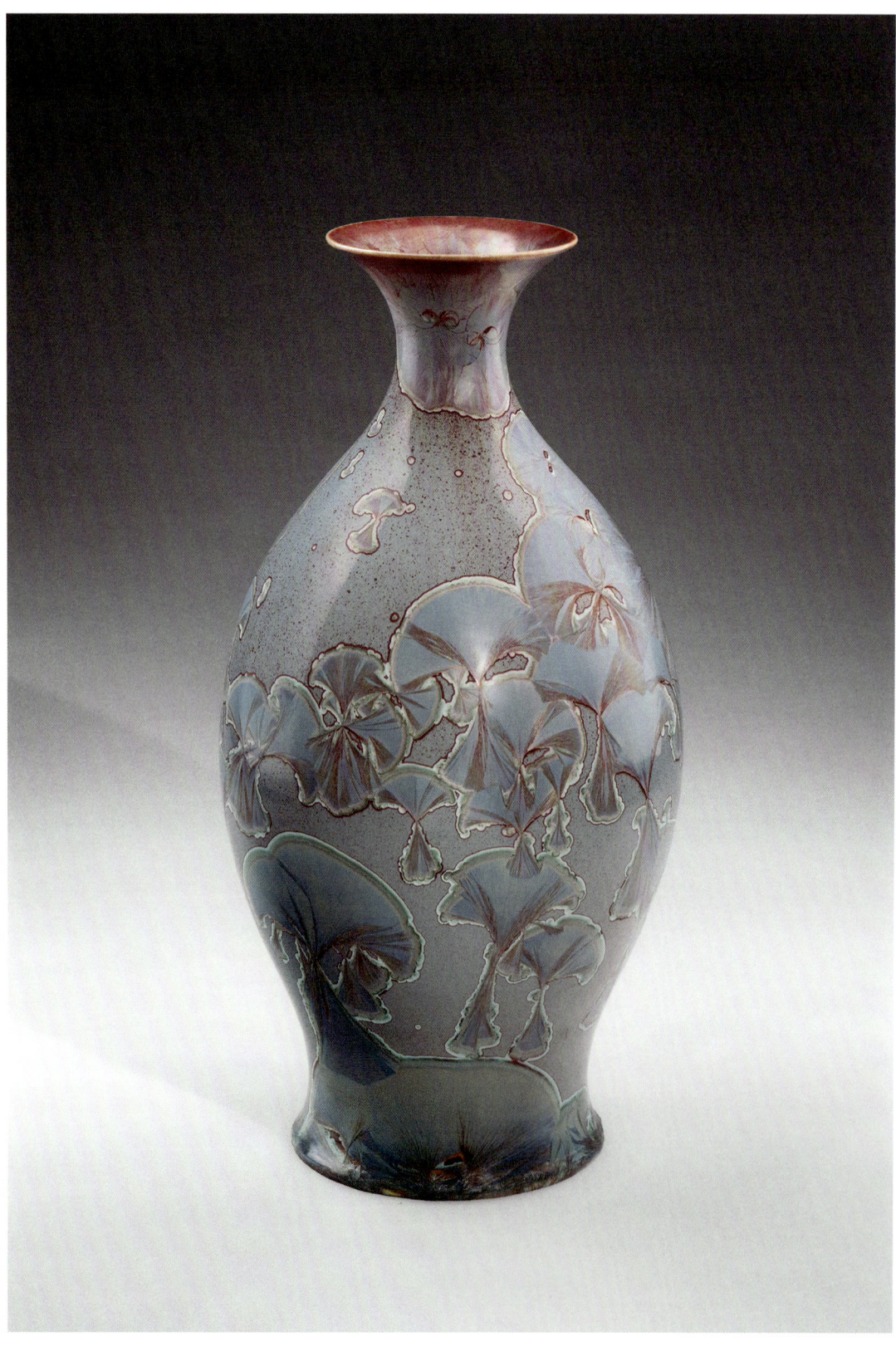

*Fig. 5: Li Hongwei,* Olive Vase, *2017, porcelain, 8 x 8 x 17 inches.*

things to come. What I noticed for the most part was a battery of glaze tests and materials, a potter's wheel and a rather small electric kiln. Hongwei was working on his investigation of crystalline glaze begun in graduate school. Step by step this investigation and the form and surface integration he sought became abundantly clear. Honoring the rich history of pottery form and glaze achievements of ancient China he perfected a language of reflection on the luxurious vessel. His distinctive eye and disciplined enjoyment of a skilled exploration of form in space produced the definitive pot as a celebration that introduces his exhibition at the Alfred Ceramic Art Museum. This work is a leading contemporary reflection on classic pottery as an artform. This is not mimicry. Far from imitation, these pots are fresh, exquisite statements of a maker's art. The word mimicry suggests to me an academic-studied efficiency. Li's pots are masterfully attentive to the sensuality of his materials. With a quality of ease and abundance his vessels echo a history of opulence as they blend surface and form into a resonate state of wonder. (Fig. 5)

Subsequent studios in West Beijing were larger. I visited a studio in West Beijing from which we traveled into the mountains referred to as the Fragrant Hills. In this studio I notice for the first time thousands of ceramic shards. Realizing that the crystalline glaze investigations produced many unsuccessful results, at first the shards seemed simply fundamental to a ceramic artist's process of critique. However, Li was recycling these shards into new works of sculpture.

What I saw in Li Hongwei's studio that day was a pragmatic caring and concern for inevitable waste associated with the ceramic process. This concern led to a possibility befitting the moment. However, I hesitated to assume that the reason behind this move toward sculpture was to intentionally establish an analogy to the chaos and detritus of the contemporary world or the purposeful demolition of the past. Thinking of the awareness and concern for process and waste encourages the thought that there is an overlapping of pragmatic intention and a deep intuitive sensitivity to the artist's time in history. Li Hongwei speaks of freedom. I think of the artist's need to free oneself from past work, to move to new challenges, to find what is next. An artist's aspirations and the potential of analogies may certainly coincide. The demolition of the past has more than one interpretation. Artists proceed to embrace making by following the process and the materials as they lead the way to a reflection on results. There is then a pause during which a recognition of conceptual complexities may arise. Next there is a move forward with renewed awareness and purpose. This activity is the *raison d'être* of being alive for the artist. (Fig. 6)

The analytical discourse of artistic intention may arise from answering the question: Why this art now? This question is a consideration of a sociological frame of reference. All artists are immersed in their time. The "reveal" associated with the art, consciously intended or

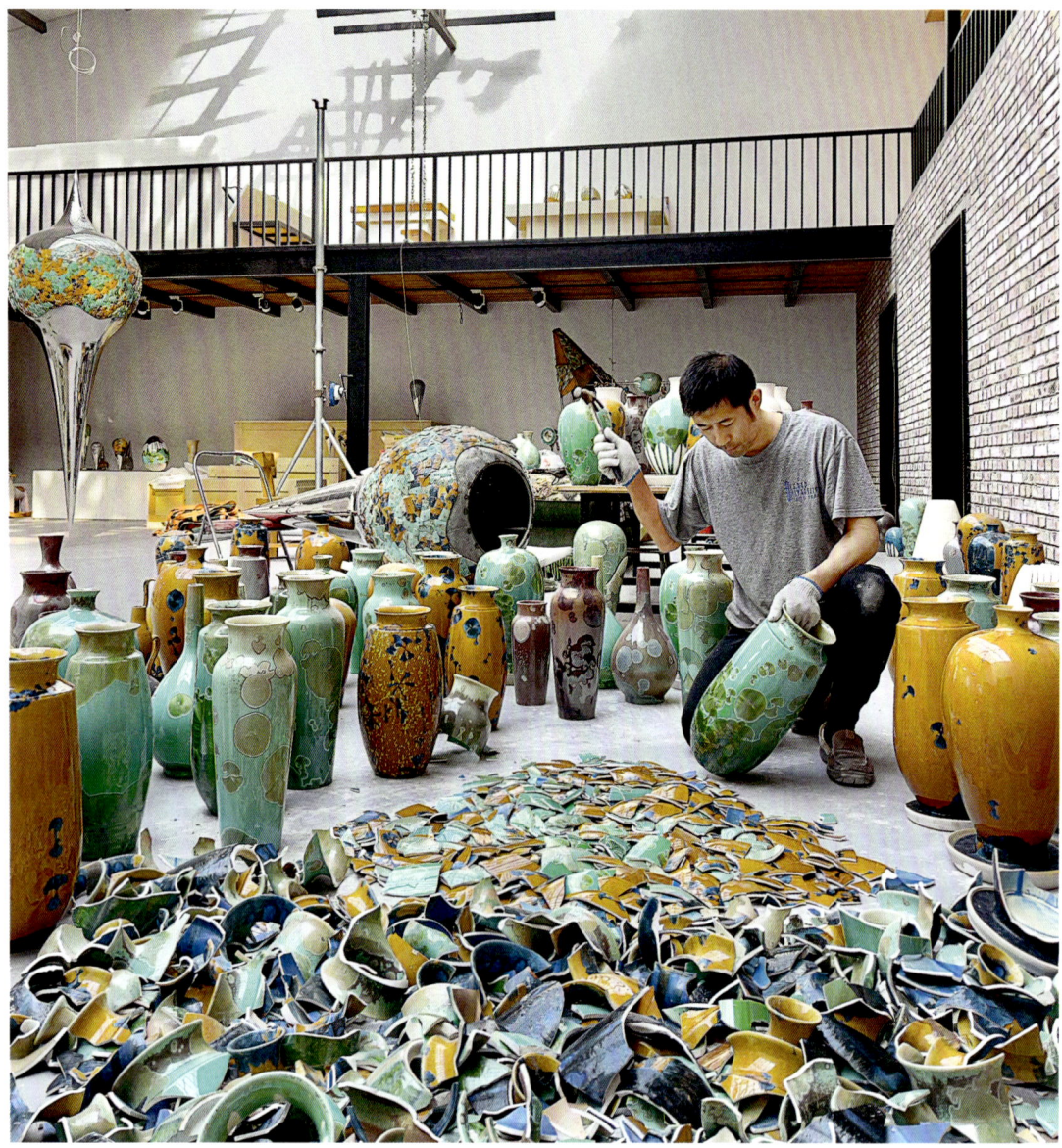

*Fig. 6: Li Hongwei, 2022, making porcelain shards. Li Hongwei studio, Beijing, China*

not, gives the art its significance. The audience attentive to work in its time may give art a particular reading—an understood meaning befitting presumption. However, art does not only stay embraced by its time in history. It may escape to become meaningful over and over again as it floats in the ether of human experience.

As Hongwei began to be recognized, the demand for more work space became important. His new Beijing studio, under construction when I visited there in December 2023, is magnificent. It is an immense space with white walls and massive sky light windows. (Fig. 7)

In 2012 Li Hongwei returned to Alfred to help finalize the installation of the second phase of *EarthCloud*. I had gathered a team of assistants, all Alfred ceramic art graduates, to complete the installation. Our start date was May 1, 2012. We had meetings each morning to set the day's schedule and several weeks of progress took place. Then, at one of our morning meetings, Li began the day by inviting us all to his wedding at Foster Lake, a beautiful local recreational site under the care of Alfred University. The wedding took place on the 7th day of the 7th month. It was July 2012, the year of the dragon. The dragon in Chinese lore is a powerful symbol of good fortune. The dragon is the water god—the god of clouds, thunder and rain. The dragon dwells in pools and lakes from which the dragon rises into the clouds. The dragon is of the earth and the sky.

Li Hongwei and his wife Luqing have three wonderful children. They divide their time between living in Beijing and Alfred. The cross-cultural continuum begun in 2005 by Li Hongwei has become a precious gift leading into the future.

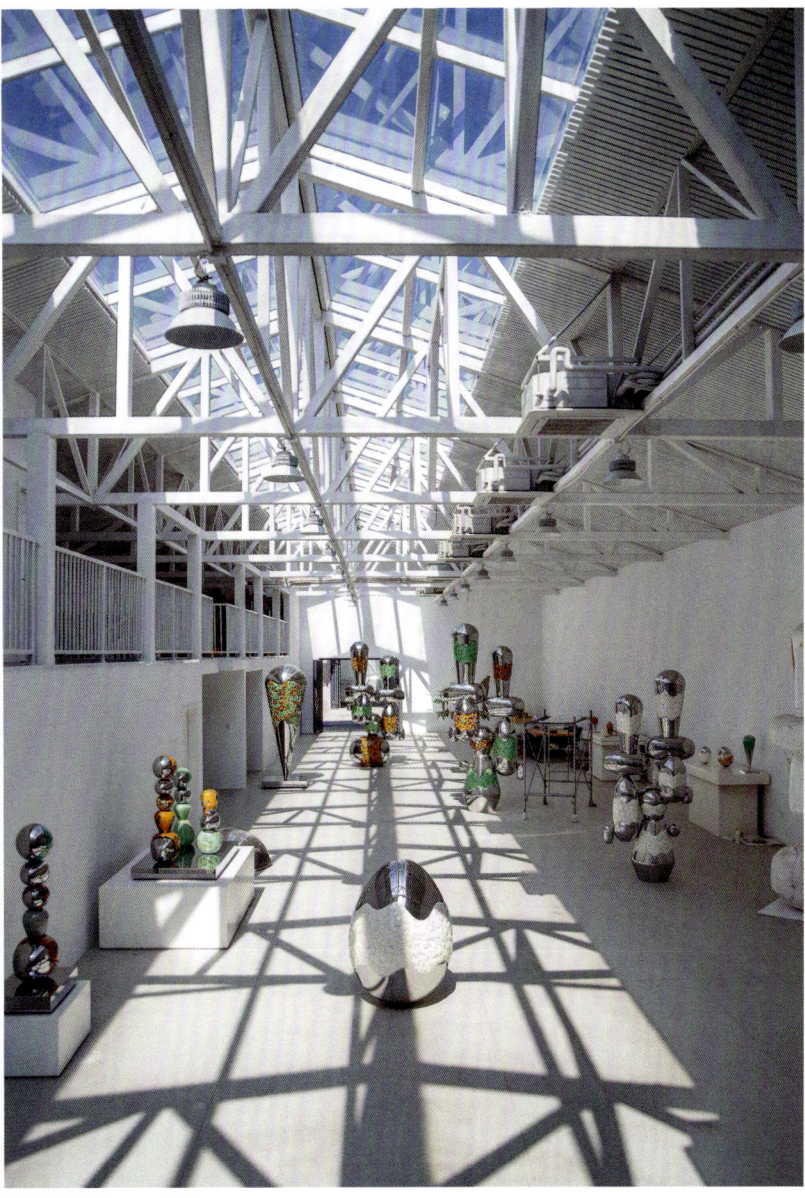

*Fig. 7: Li Hongwei, Beijing studio view with completed sculptures, 2024.*
*Photo Li Hongwei Studio Beijing, China*

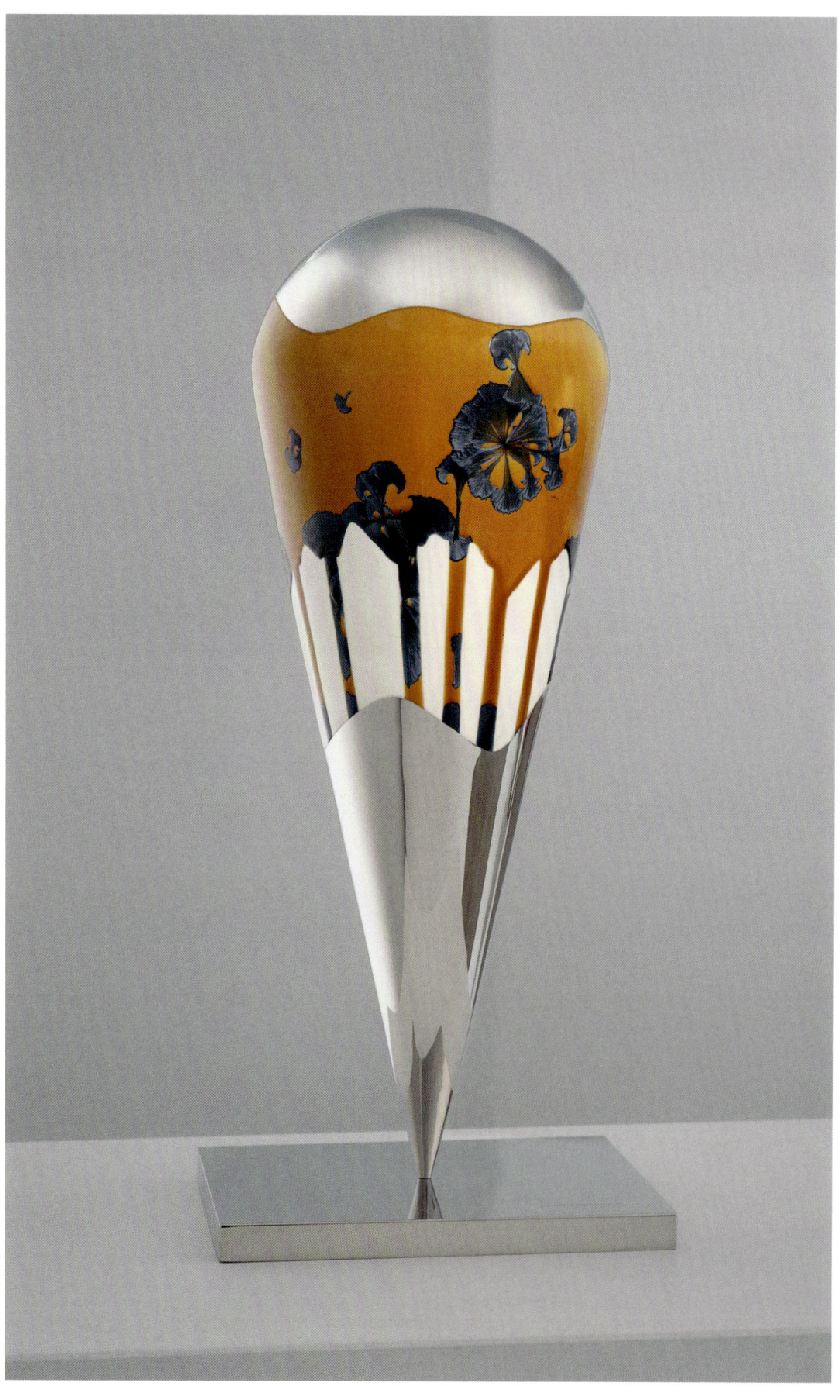

*Fig. 8: Li Hongwei,* Upwelling of Gravity #52, *2019, porcelain, stainless steel 9.8 x 9.8 x 21.7 inches.*

Because of the exhibition here at the Alfred Ceramic Art Museum, I have had the rare opportunity to spend time with Li Hongwei's art during multiple viewings. Via its outward sign Li's art proposes a place where the finite and infinite intersect. Li's sculpture simplified in the *Upwelling Gravity* series (Fig. 8) brings me to a threshold where imagination breaks the bonds of gravity. My bodily sensation brings to mind reflections on the athleticism of ballet and the late 18th century invention of the pointe shoe, devised to create the illusion that the dancers were weightless. Once while in the museum gallery experiencing Li's sculpture, I thought about Georgian-American ballet choreographer George Balanchine's brilliant choreographic formalism which often incorporates the tradition of the pointe shoe. Balanchine's style has often been described as neoclassic. I began thinking that Li has established a reimagined variation of neoclassicism comprised of his personal sense of Western tradition, Chinese philosophy and modernist abstraction. This particular alchemy consists of combining formality and order with seductive materials and technical prowess to achieve a unifying, optimistic balance of dynamic contrasts. The absolute is presented, yet only momentarily. Analogous to ballet, body movement in space allows new perspectives to continually emerge as I move around the sculpture. I see myself reflected in the work and feel myself in a vortex of vision and revision where the world of extraordinary material fact is dramatically present as an invitation to a sensual and cognitive journey beyond anything previously imagined.

Works of art lead toward contemplation. Consideration of the binding relationship between material, process and artistic purpose is necessary to grasp the bounty art offers. Li Hongwei's command of his personal vision is a major testament to a transformation of material and process into sculptural luminescence—a distinctive dimensional poetry of Radiance.

Wayne Higby

Footnotes

1. *Cultivating Dualities: A Conversation with Li Hongwei*, Michael Amy, Sculpture Magazine, International Sculpture Center, Hampton, NJ, 5/22/2019.

2. *Self-Portrait: The Art of Li Hongwei,* Wayne Higby, Beyond Reflection: The Art of Li Hongwei, Pucker Art Publications, Boston, MA ISBN 978-1-879985-37-7, 2018.

3. *Steering My Ship*, Hongwei Li, Master of Fine Arts Thesis Report, Scholes Library Archives, Alfred University, Alfred, NY, 2007.

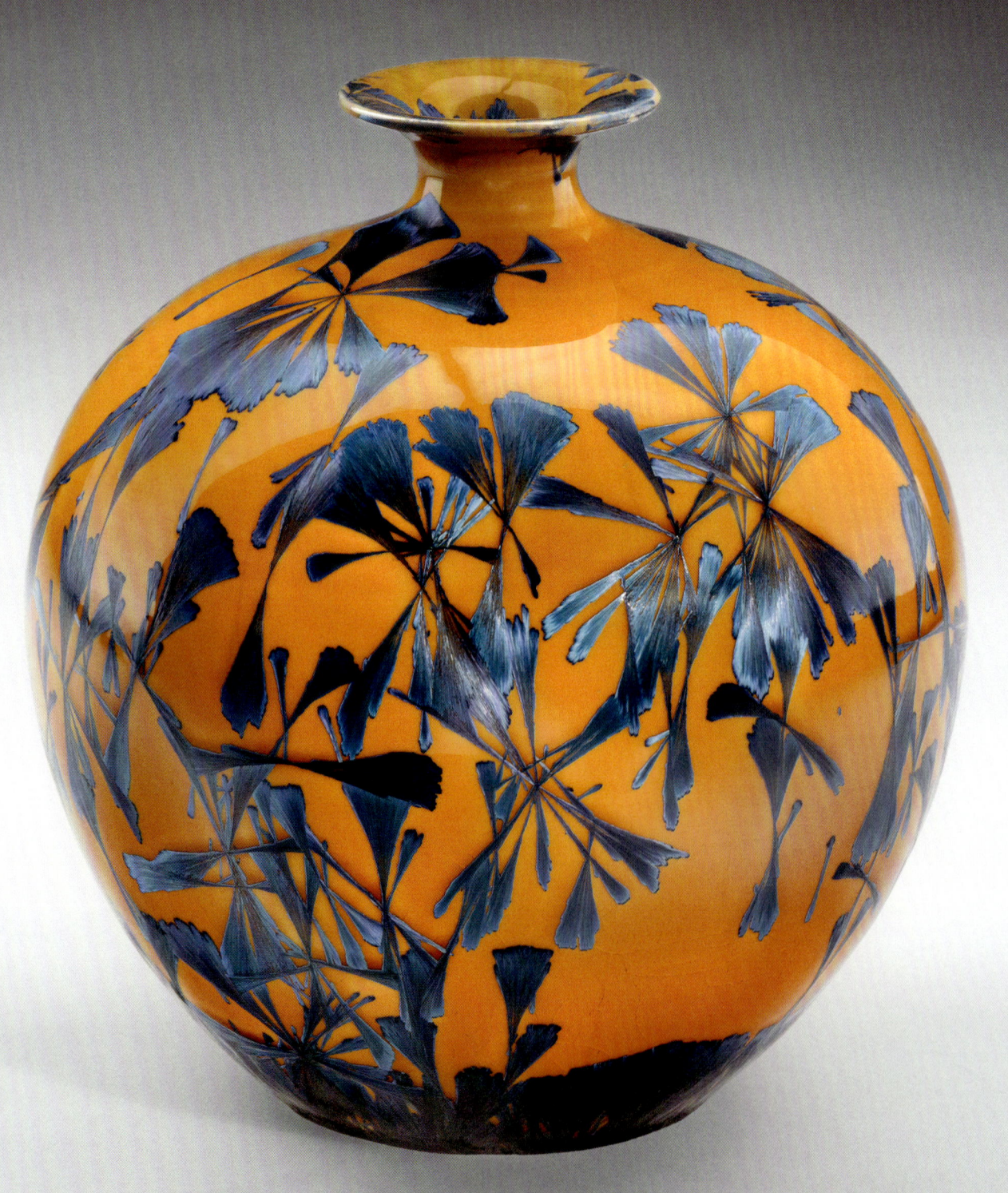

# MATERIALS, MINDFULNESS, MASTERY: THE ART OF LI HONGWEI

## DENISE PATRY LEIDY

One of the most innovative and thoughtful ceramicists working today, Li Hongwei embodies longstanding Chinese perceptions regarding the role of art, and the nature of artistic practice. Calligraphers and painters, the most valued artists in Chinese history, were often extolled for their knowledge of earlier compositions and brush strokes. A meaningful work of art was expected to quote or emulate these styles, sometimes responding with original themes and new types of brushstrokes, but that was secondary to the display of historical knowledge. Brushing a painting or a calligraphy rooted in history, philosophy, and literature was viewed as a method of self-reflection and development. Works of art lacking such underpinnings have traditionally (though not always accurately) been judged to be lesser creations. Although similar concepts are found in the West, usually again primarily associated with painting, these concepts appear much earlier in Chinese culture.

*Li Hongwei,* Pomegranate Vase*, 2017, porcelain, 8.7 x 8.7 x 8.7 inches.*

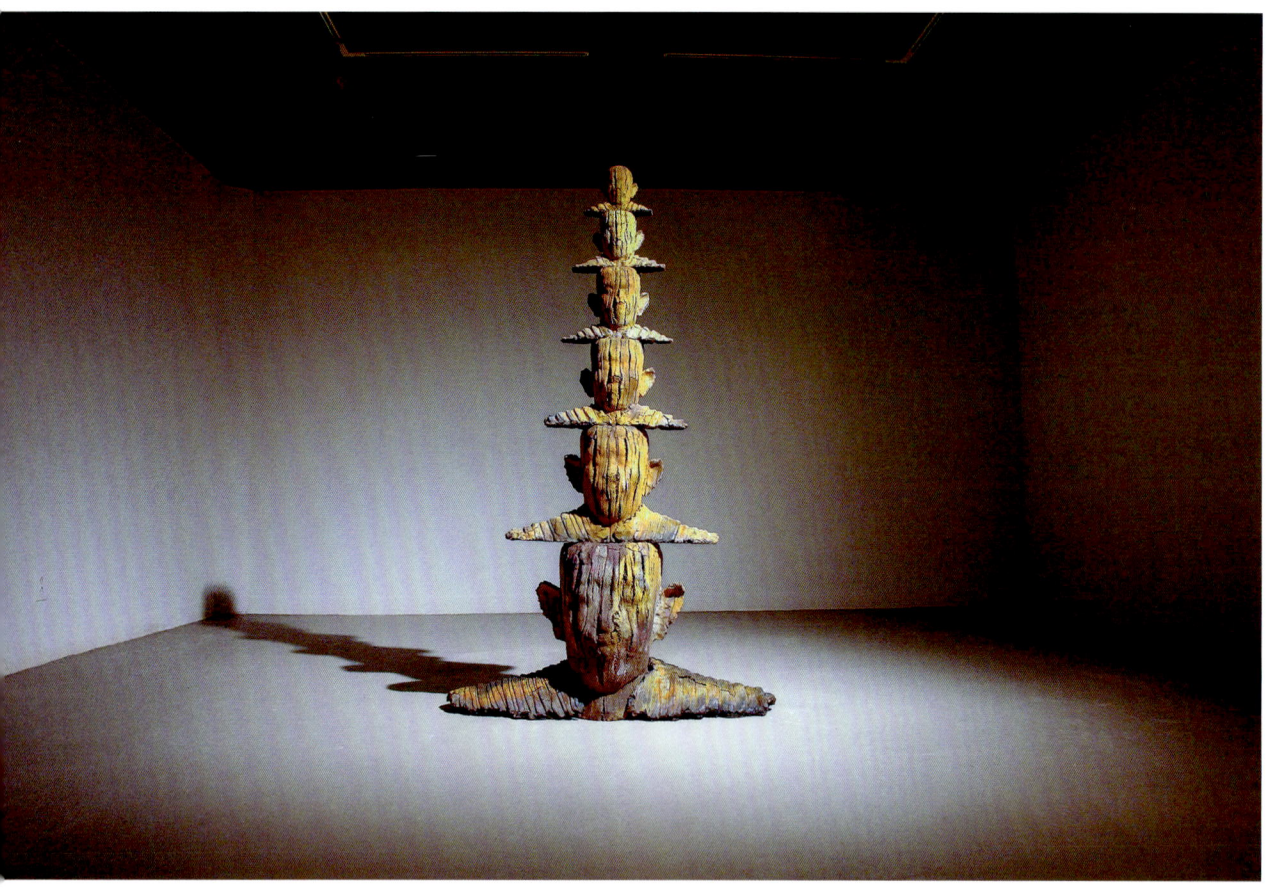

Fig. 1: Li Hongwei (Chinese Born 1980), Weight of Meditation #2, 2006, H. 43 inches,
Alfred Ceramic Art Museum, 2007.4. Photo: Li Hongwei archive

Li, who was introduced to painting and calligraphy in his home in Shandong Province,
before studying at the Central Academy of Art in Beijing, follows this tradition using clay,
particularly porcelain, to explore forms, ideas, and his place in the world around him while
also celebrating China's preeminence in global ceramic history. Works from his *Weight
of Meditation* (Fig. 1) series, among the first pieces he produced as a student at Alfred
University, explore his identity, and the inherent challenges of a Chinese student in an
American university while working with the American version of Japanese raku. The
sculpture, crafted with a fired clay, prefigures many of the concerns that are highlighted in
works produced throughout his career: an interest in scale, the layering and repurposing
of shapes, and a fascination with surfaces. The latter is evident in the strips of clay that
partially cover the faces in the work while hinting at the underlying substructure, enlivening
the sculpture, and capturing a viewer's attention.

Li's ceramics often interpret earlier Chinese shapes, which have their own nuanced
histories and symbolism. For example, a *meiping* or plum vase (Fig. 2) echoes a vessel
that first appeared in the Chinese repertory in the eleventh and twelfth centuries (Fig. 3).
Initially known as a *jingping* or bottle with straight neck, by the seventeenth century this
shape was also used to display a blossoming plum branch, a harbinger of spring, and

22

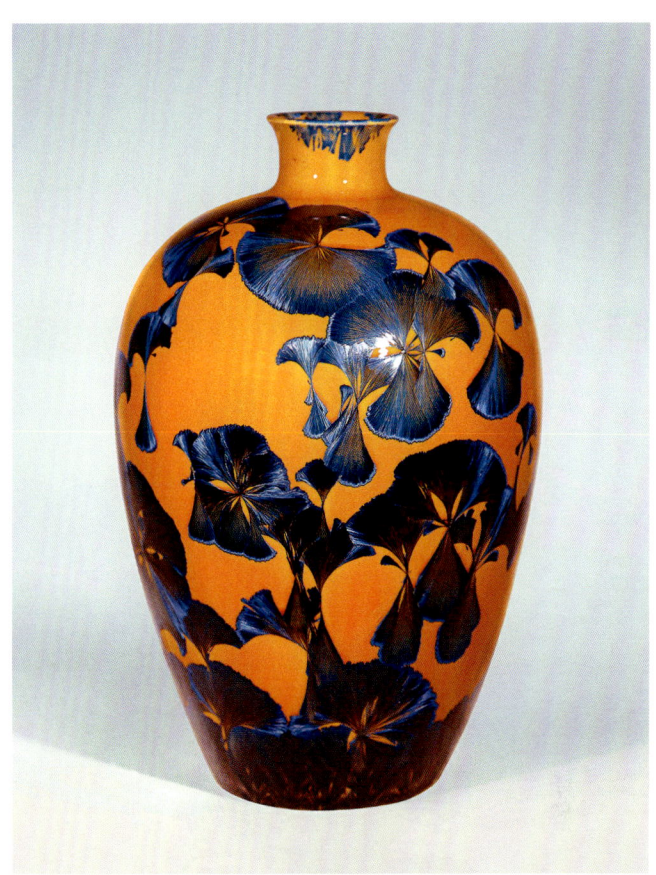

*Fig. 2: Li Hongwei,* Meiping Vase, *porcelain with splashed peacock glaze, H. 15 ½ inches, Image Courtesy Pucker Gallery (HL165)*

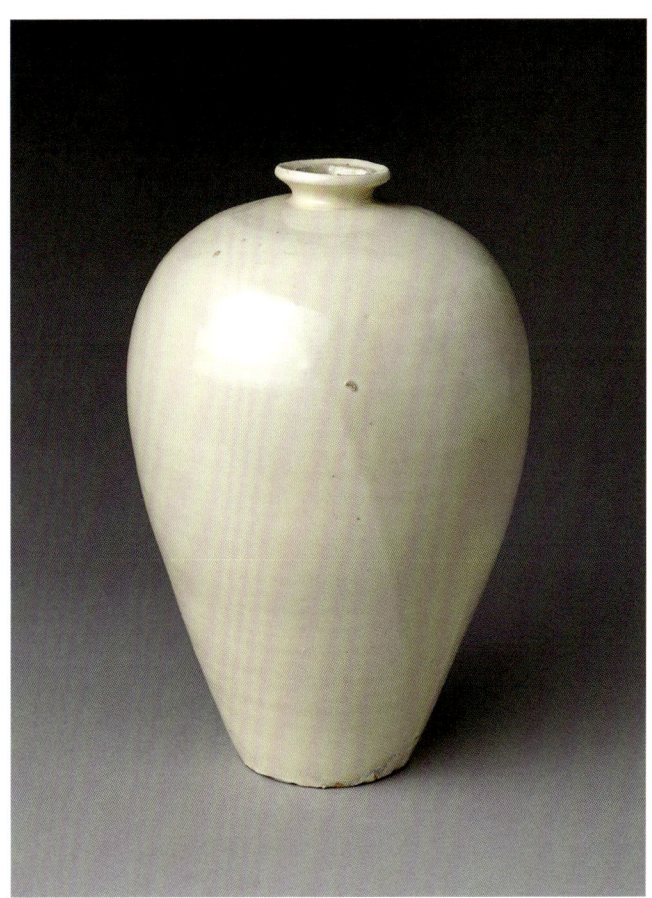

*Fig. 3:* Bottle in Meiping Shape, *China, Northern Song dynasty (960 – 1127), 11th – 12th century stoneware with white glaze (Cizhou ware), H. 11 3/8 inches, Rogers Fund, 1922 (22.91.1), The Metropolitan Museum of Art*

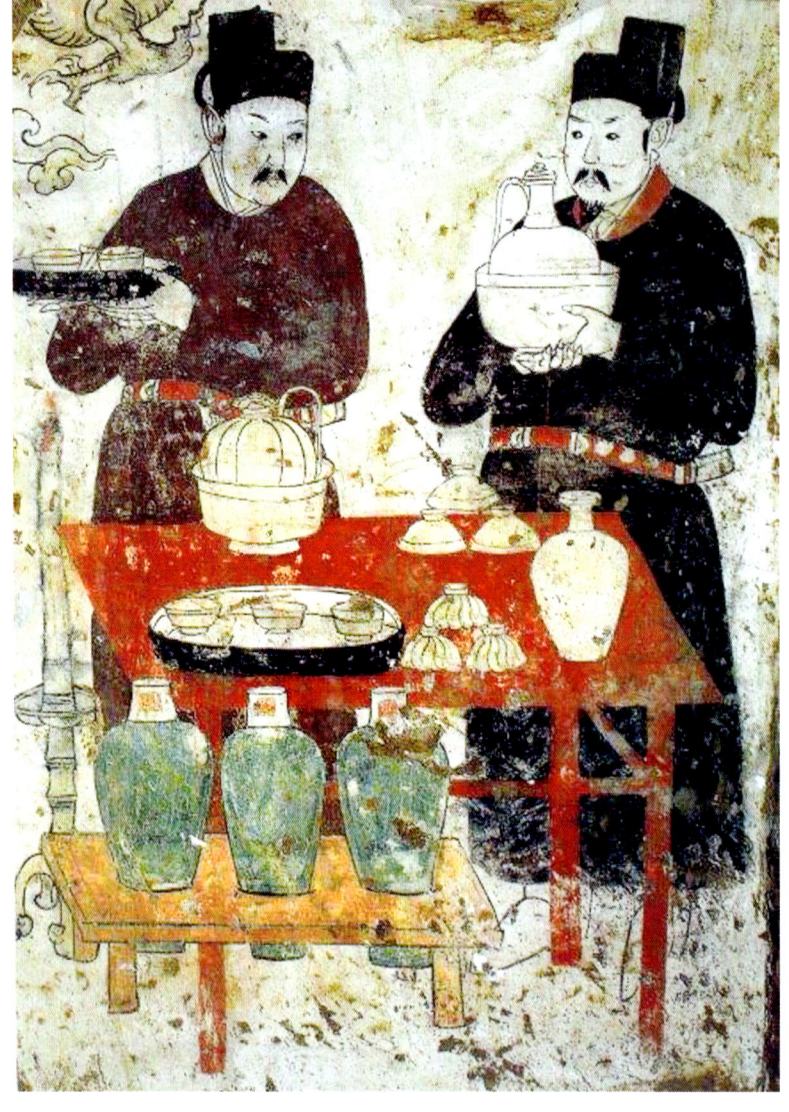

Fig. 4: Banquet Preparation, *detail from a mural in the tomb of Zhang Shiping (d. 1116). Water based pigment over clay mixed with sand.*

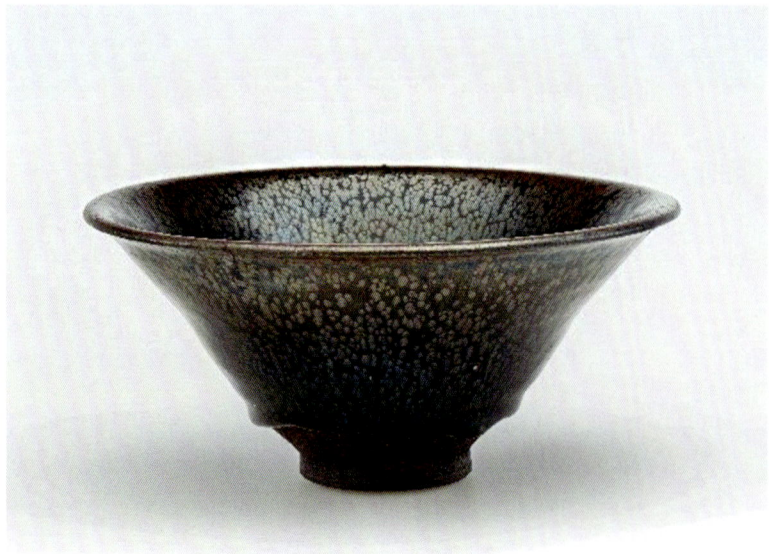

Fig. 5: Tea Bowl, *China, Southern Song dynasty (1127 – 1278), 12th – 13th century, stoneware with oil spot glaze (Jian ware), Diam. 7 9/16 inches (19.2 cm), Gift of Charles Lang Freer (F1909.369.004), The Freer Gallery, Smithsonian, The National Museum of Asian Art*

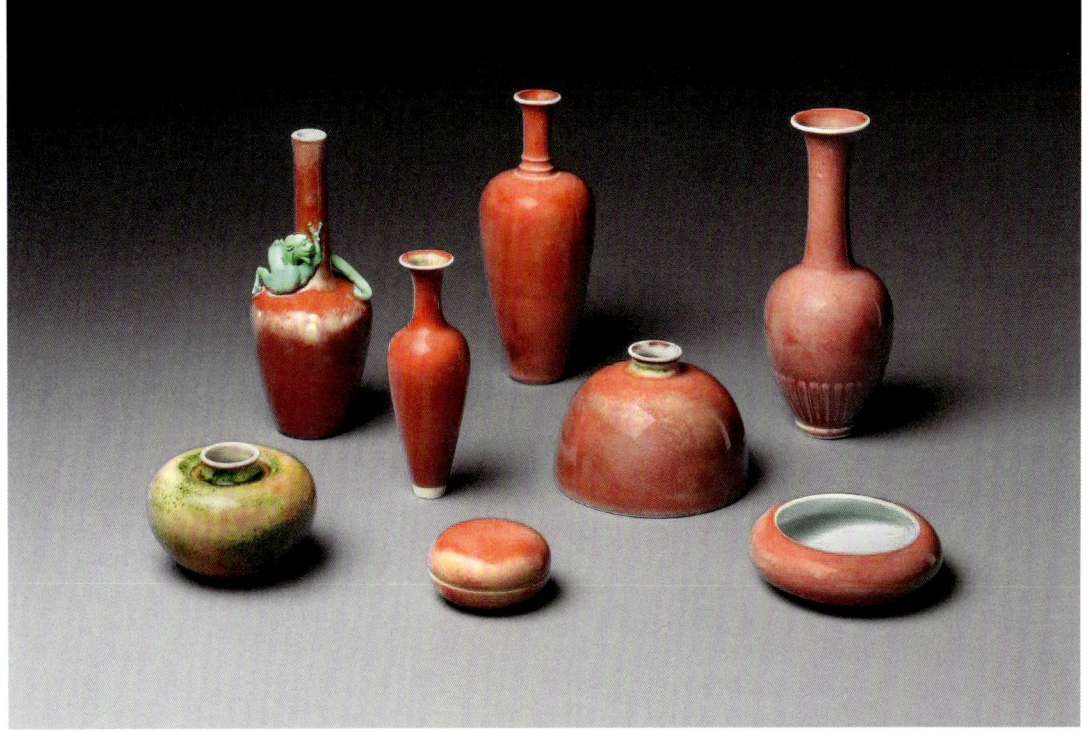

Fig. 6: Objects for a Scholar's Desk, *China, Qing dynasty (1644 – 1911), Kangxi period (1662 – 1722), Porcelain with peach bloom glaze, H. 2 ⅞ – 8 ¾ inches*
*Left to right:* Water Coupe, *H.O. Havemeyer Collection, Bequest of Mrs. H.O. Havemeyer, 1929 (29.100.33);* Vase with Dragon, Vase, *and* Seal Paste Box, *Bequest of Benjamin Altman, 1913 (14.40.362., 381., 369);* Vase, *Bequest of Mary Stilmann Harknesss, 1950 (50.142.286);* Water Coupe and Vase, *Gift of Edwin C. Vogel, 1965 (65.225.3.,5);* Brush Washer, *H. O. Havemeyer Collection, Bequest of Mrs. H. O. Havemeyer, 1929 (29.100.352), The Metropolitan Museum of Art*

symbol of resilience. The *meiping*, which developed to store and serve distilled, as opposed to fermented, wine, evolved when the Chinese ceramic industry was flourishing, with thousands of kilns producing wares for the court, for domestic use, and for trade. Murals painted in tombs from this period (Fig. 4), which often feature preparations for drinking wine and tea, attest to the popularity of these activities in many strata of society from the tenth to the thirteenth centuries.

The lush peacock blue crystals also derive from earlier Chinese traditions. The first use of crystalline glazes can be traced to kilns working in Fujian Province during the twelfth and thirteenth centuries when iron oxide in the glaze covering a tea bowl would precipitate to the surface to create astonishing patterns such as hare's fur and oil spot (Fig. 5). Tea bowls with such glazes, particularly those made in the Jian kilns, have played a fascinating role in global ceramic history.  Some were traded to Japan: others brought there by Buddhist monks who traveled to China to study with famed monks.  Five such Chinese tea bowls are designated as Japanese National Treasures, a testament to their historical and cultural importance. Moreover, tea bowls of this type made in both China and later Japan, and often designated by the Japanese word *tenmoku*, were introduced to the west in the late nineteenth and early twentieth century as part of the interest in Japanese ceramics that underlies the Arts and Crafts Movement (1880 – 1910). Appreciation for the work of potters, often inspired by East Asian ceramics, expanded in the West at that time.

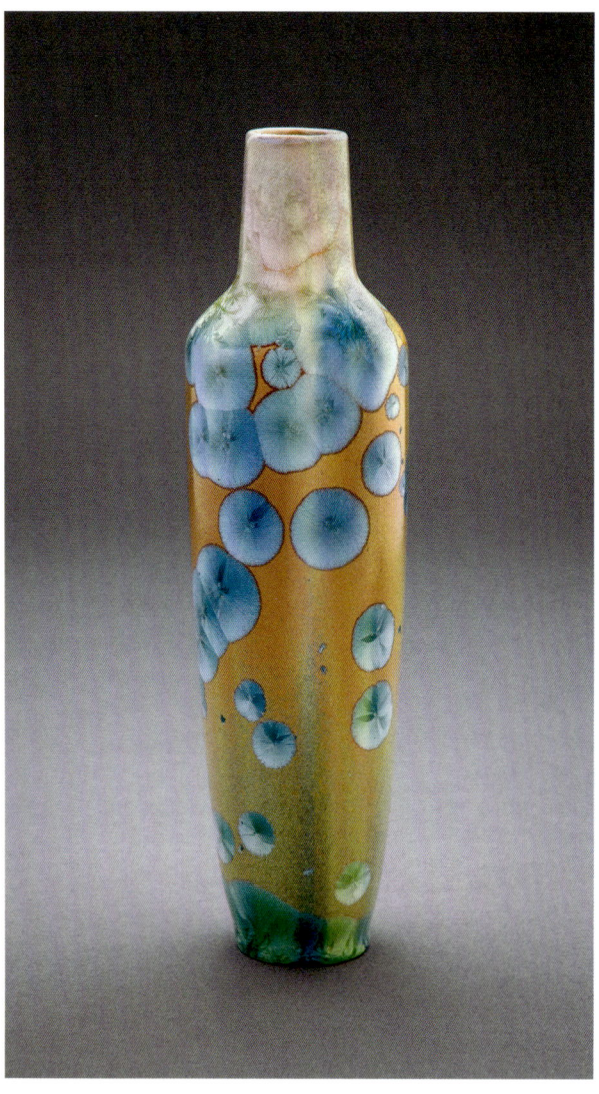

*Fig. 7: Taxile Doat (French, 1851 – 1938), Vase, 1913, porcelain with glaze, H. 9 ¾ inches, Gift of Leeds Art Foundation in honor or Brent R. Benjamin (331.2020), The Saint Louis Museum of Art*

The challenging crystalline glazes reappear in China in the late sixteenth and early seventeenth centuries, a period of experimentation in the great complex at Jingdezhen in Jiangxi Province. By this time, Jingdezhen, nicknamed the "porcelain city," had become the predominant center in China replacing most of the kilns active earlier in both the north and the south. Initially, the lush but delicate crystalline peach bloom glaze was reserved for a group of eight small items (Fig. 6) used by scholar officials who ran the government bureaucracy, many of whom were also famed calligraphers and painters. Peach bloom, and other seventeenth and eighteenth century high-fired glazes, such as oxblood (*sang-de-boeuf*) or moonlight (*clair-de-lune*), become known in Europe after the seventeenth century due to the overwhelming extent of global trade in Chinese porcelain at the time. By the late nineteenth century, ceramicists such as the French Taxile Doat (1851 – 1939) were experimenting with high-fired or *grand feu* ceramics creating variants of these extraordinary glazes including works with crystal patterns. (Fig. 7). It is interesting to note that Doat was one of three specialists hired in 1909 by the Art Academy and Porcelain Works in Missouri to help spur the American ceramic industry, a decade after the English-born Charles Fergus Binns (1857 – 1934) became the founding director of the New York State College of Clayworking and Ceramics at Alfred University, established for the same purpose. Although crystalline glazes were popular in western ceramics in the late nineteenth and early twentieth century, they disappeared after World War I, possibly due to the costs and the difficulty in making them, but became popular again in the late twentieth and early twenty-first century.

Like the peacock blue on the *meiping* discussed above, the lush but delicate crystalline green forms (Fig. 7) on *Upwelling of Gravity #3* (Fig. 8) appear to exist beyond the surface of the clay, adding movement and vitality to the sculpture. The Chinese language title (li岦) for works in this series translates as high mountains, but is also a homonym for strength and power (力), and the process of erecting or building (立). In English, "upwelling of gravity" refers to an event when colder, denser water rises to the surface of a body of water, an apt metaphor for the process and effect of Li's unique glazes. While the upper part of Upwelling of Gravity is crafted with porcelain—a Chinese invention from the seventh century— the lower section of this sculpture is made with stainless steel, a hallmark of the industrial revolution invented in the early nineteenth century. Stainless steel shares the reflective nature of a glaze but allows a viewer to see himself/herself in this work of art, adding visual depth and an interactive element to Li's work.

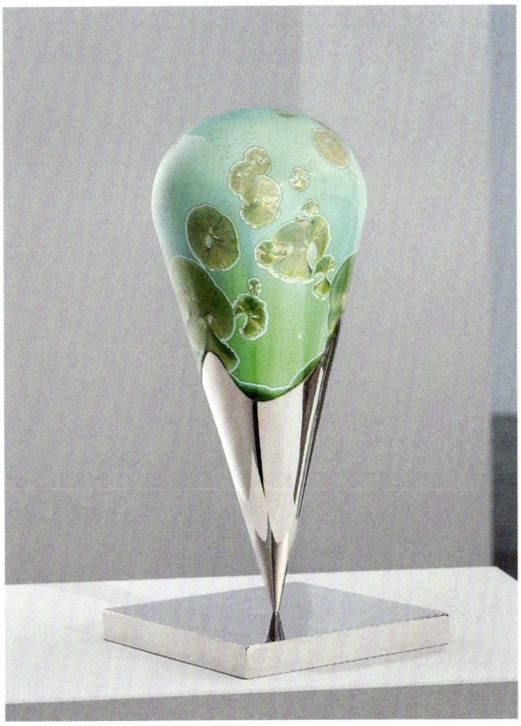

*Fig. 8: Li Hongwei,* Upwelling of Gravity #3, *2017, porcelain, stainless steel, H. 21 inches*

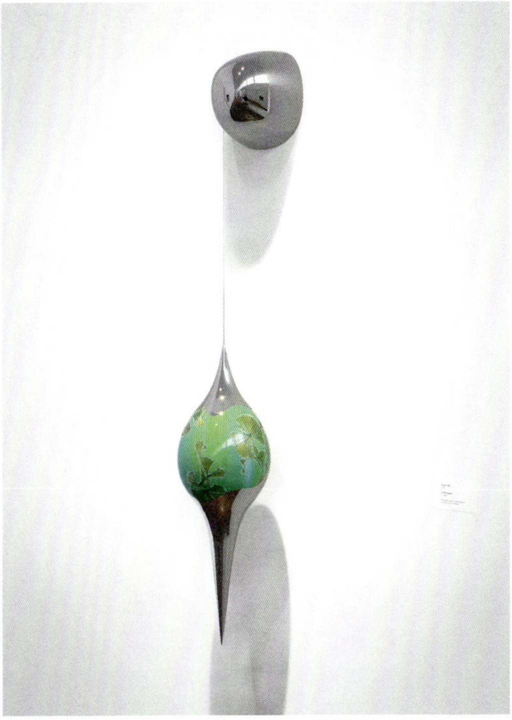

*Fig. 9: Li Hongwei,* Xuan #30, *2021, porcelain, stainless steel, H. 28 ½ inches*

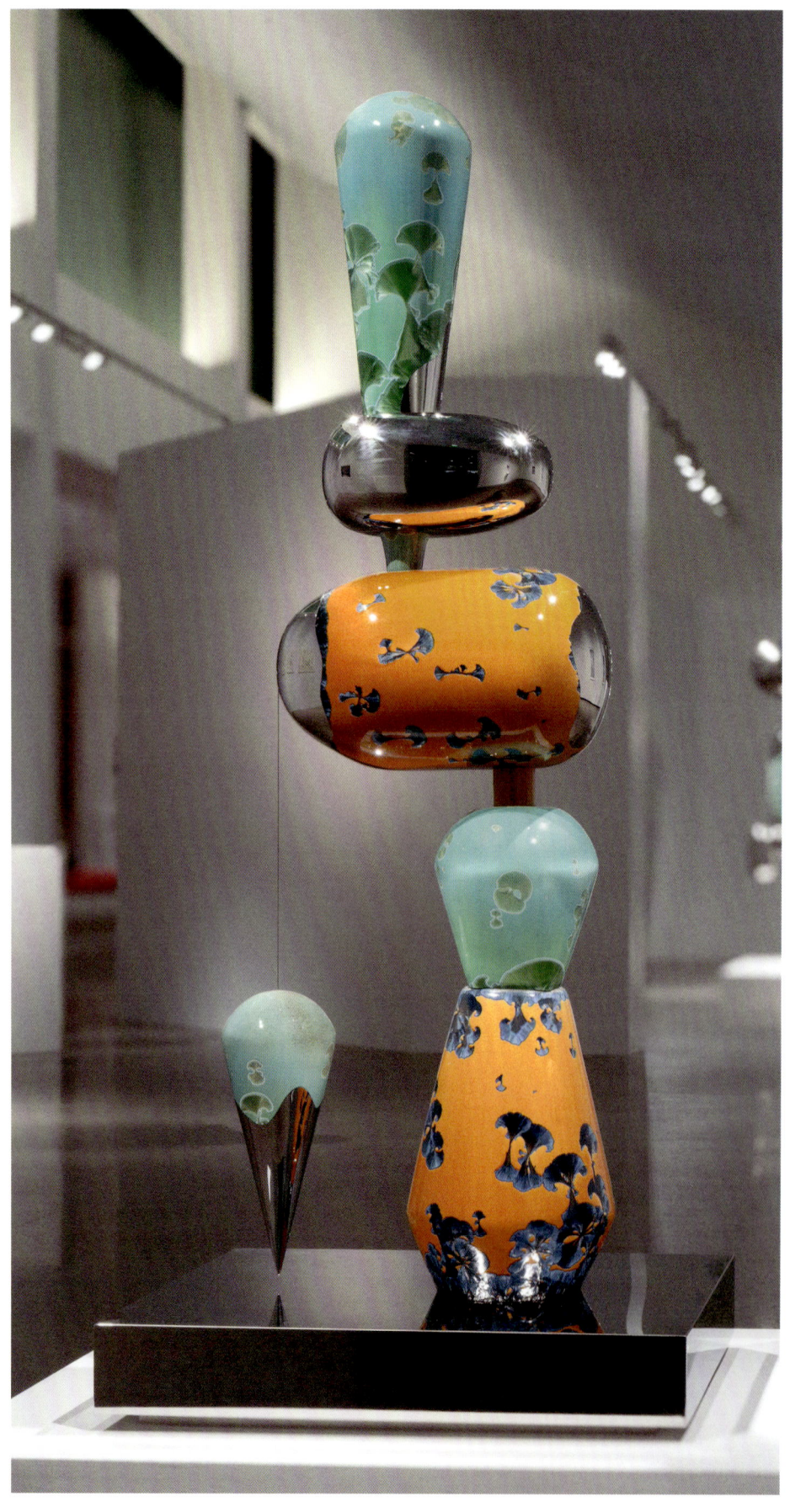

*Fig. 10: Li Hongwei,* Allegory of Balance #41, *porcelain, stainless steel, H. 63 inches*

Li Hongwei began to experiment with stainless steel in 2009 and successfully incorporated it into his work in 2014. *Xuan #30* (Fig. 9), which also takes the form of a liquid drop, and is covered with his characteristic green "traces of ink," glaze (an echo of the shades of green favored in the Chinese celadons of the tenth to the fourteenth century), further attests to his astonishing melding of these two distinct materials. *Xuan* (玄), the Chinese character for the title of the works in this series can be traced to the *Daodejing* (or *Tao Te Ching*, "The Way and Its Power"), the seminal text for the practice of *Daoism. Daoism*, which derives from the character *dao*, meaning way or path, is a term for longstanding beliefs and practices, which coalesced during the second and fourth century. *Daoism* includes metaphysical and philosophical speculations, the ability to become a fully realized individual or a sage, and the quest for mundane benefits such as wealth and fame. In the *Daodejing*, the character *Xuan* means mysterious, and implies the exploration of mystery. The Chinese language lends itself to homonyms and puns: another character that is also pronounced *xuan* (悬) connotes hanging and suspension, an accurate description of the use of a thin wire to suspend and display this, and other works, in the series. Homonyms are often found in the decoration of Chinese porcelains after the seventeenth century. For example, the popular theme of flying bats (蝠) is an allusion to and a wish for wealth (富). The characters for both words are pronounced *fu*.

The delightful drop shapes found in both *Upwelling of Gravity* and *Xuan*, as well as the distinctive gold and blue, and green glazes, are also featured in *Allegory of Balance #41* (Fig. 10). In this series, Li reinterprets and refocuses his visual language, melding beautifully crafted and glazed porcelain shapes with other equally well-made pieces in stainless steel. Li and his assistants make each element individually before carefully assembling the finished work, at which point the steel elements are usually fitted to the porcelain pieces. *Allegory of Balance #41* further illustrates Li's study of the *Daodejing* and other philosophical treatises. This sculpture combines shapes, materials, and surfaces, a melding of elements that alludes to the Daoist concept of yin and yang. Yin, associated with the female, earth, the moon, and darkness, and yang, symbolic of the male, the heavens, the sun, and light, are in a constant state of transformation and balance. The unexpected juxtapositions of shapes and patterns to create *Allegory of Balance #41* beautifully illustrate the yin-yang symbiosis, which is at the heart of the cosmos, and the basis of our daily lives.

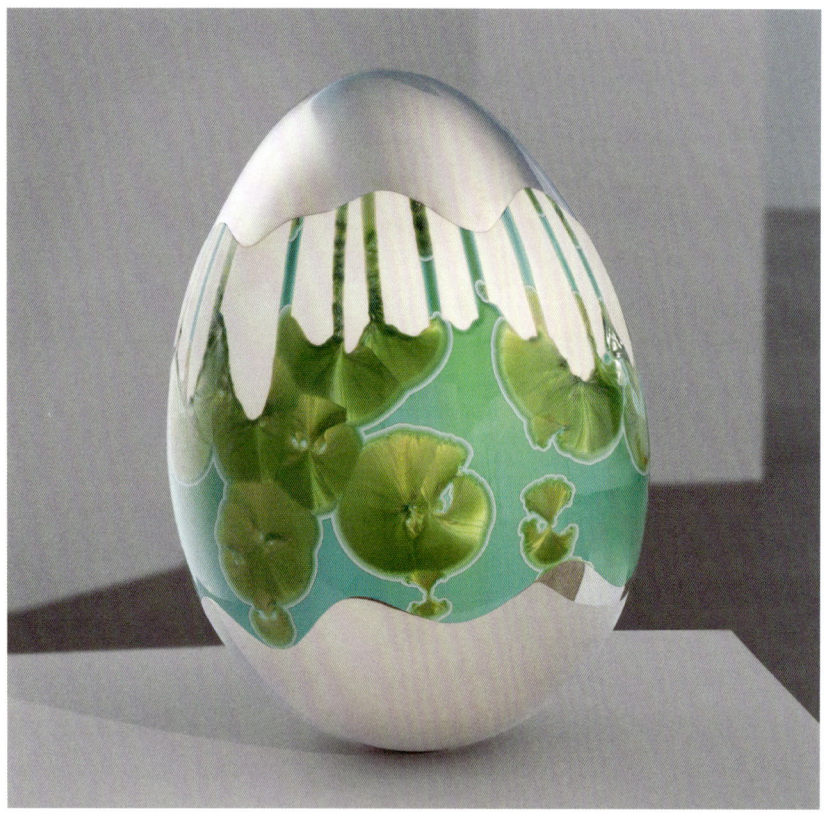

*Fig. 11: Li Hongwei,* Dan #12, *2022, porcelain, stainless steel H. 19 inches.*

Balance, transformation, and interconnectivity also inform the seemingly precarious sculptures in the *Dan* series. *Dan #12* (Fig. 11) is crafted with a green-glazed porcelain in the center, and two stainless steels caps, perfectly melded to fit the shape of the porcelain, at the ends. The darker organic green crystals, suggestive of gingko leaves or some other foliage, which precipitate from the light blue-green glaze, appear to be suspended from the narrow stems that fall from the edges of the steel cap at the upper edge of the piece. The Daodejing, which speaks of something undefined coming into existence before Heaven and Earth, once again informs pieces in this series. Moreover, the title *"Dan"* refers to the Chinese character for egg (蛋), as well as those for birth (誕) and dawn (旦), which are pronounced the same way. All three words, in both Chinese and English, allude to new beginnings of the cosmos, days, and individuals.

Another tilted egg-shaped piece *The Origins #7* (Fig. 12) has a center sculpted with broken fragments of glazed porcelain that are held together with stainless steel screws attached to underlying sheets of stainless steel. Potters have discarded imperfectly shaped or fired pieces for millennia. As ceramic became more important and valued everywhere, partially in response to widespread use of Chinese porcelain, however, broken pieces were more likely to be conserved. This is particularly true in Japan where, beginning in the sixteenth

30

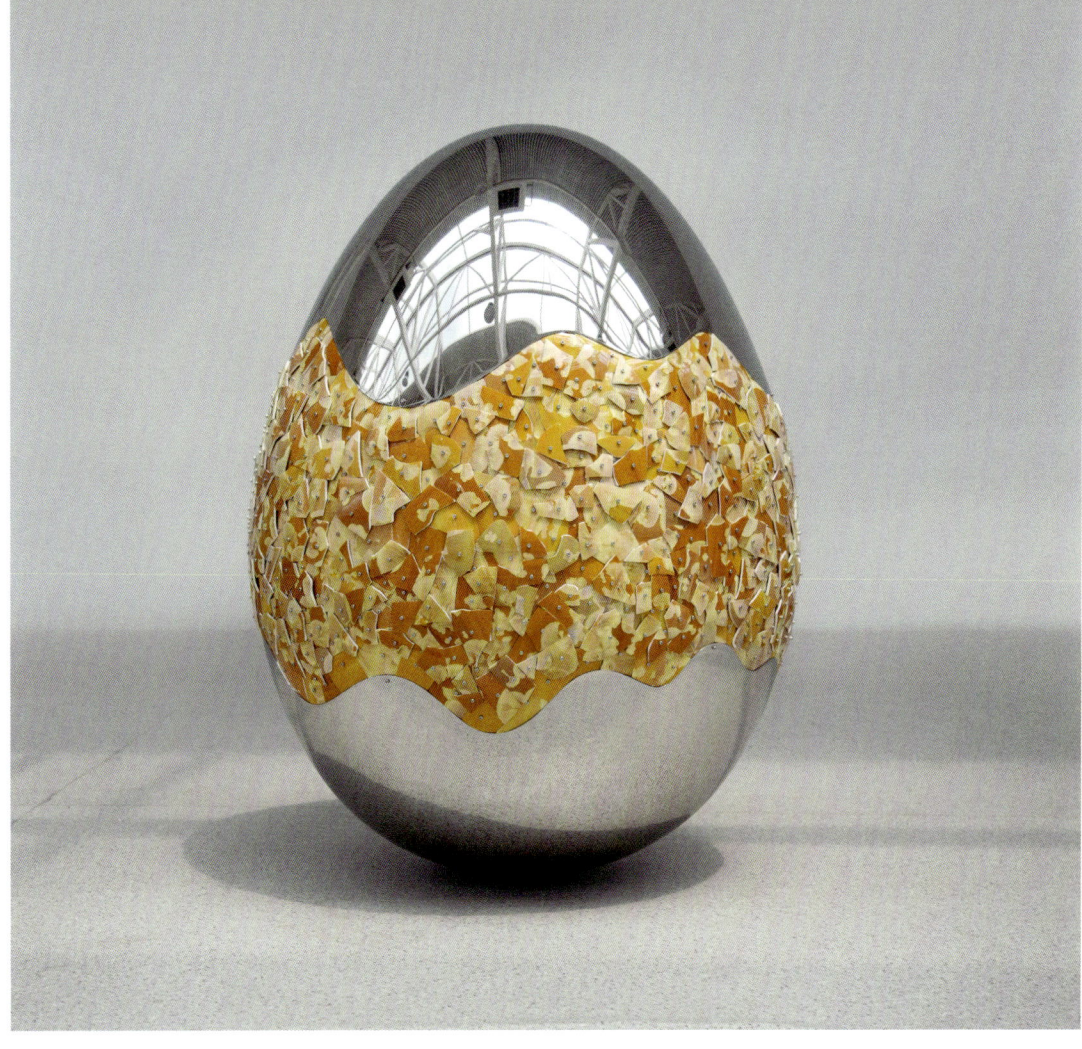

*Fig. 12: Li Hongwei,* The Origin #7, *2021, porcelain, stainless steel, H. 35 ½ inches. Image courtesy Pucker Safrai Gallery*

century, gold lacquer (known as *kintsugi*) was used to repair and preserve cherished ceramics, often works imported from China that were particularly treasured. Li, who also initially discarded damaged or less-than-perfect pieces, chooses to give these bits new life by incorporating them into his work.

The porcelain bits at the heart of *The Origins #7* illustrate an interest in layering long highlighted in Li's work: It can be seen in the crystalline patterns that dance in the glazes, the combining of materials, and the juxtaposition of disparate forms. During an interview at the Kalamazoo Institute of Art in 2022, Li explained that he started working with these fragments as a response to his growing awareness of the conflicts in the United States as he traveled throughout the country just before the pandemic in 2019. He reunites these bits, symbolic of destruction, damage, and brokenness to make masterful pieces that serve as signposts and advocates for the creativity, balance, and harmony much needed in the world today.

Denise Patry Leidy

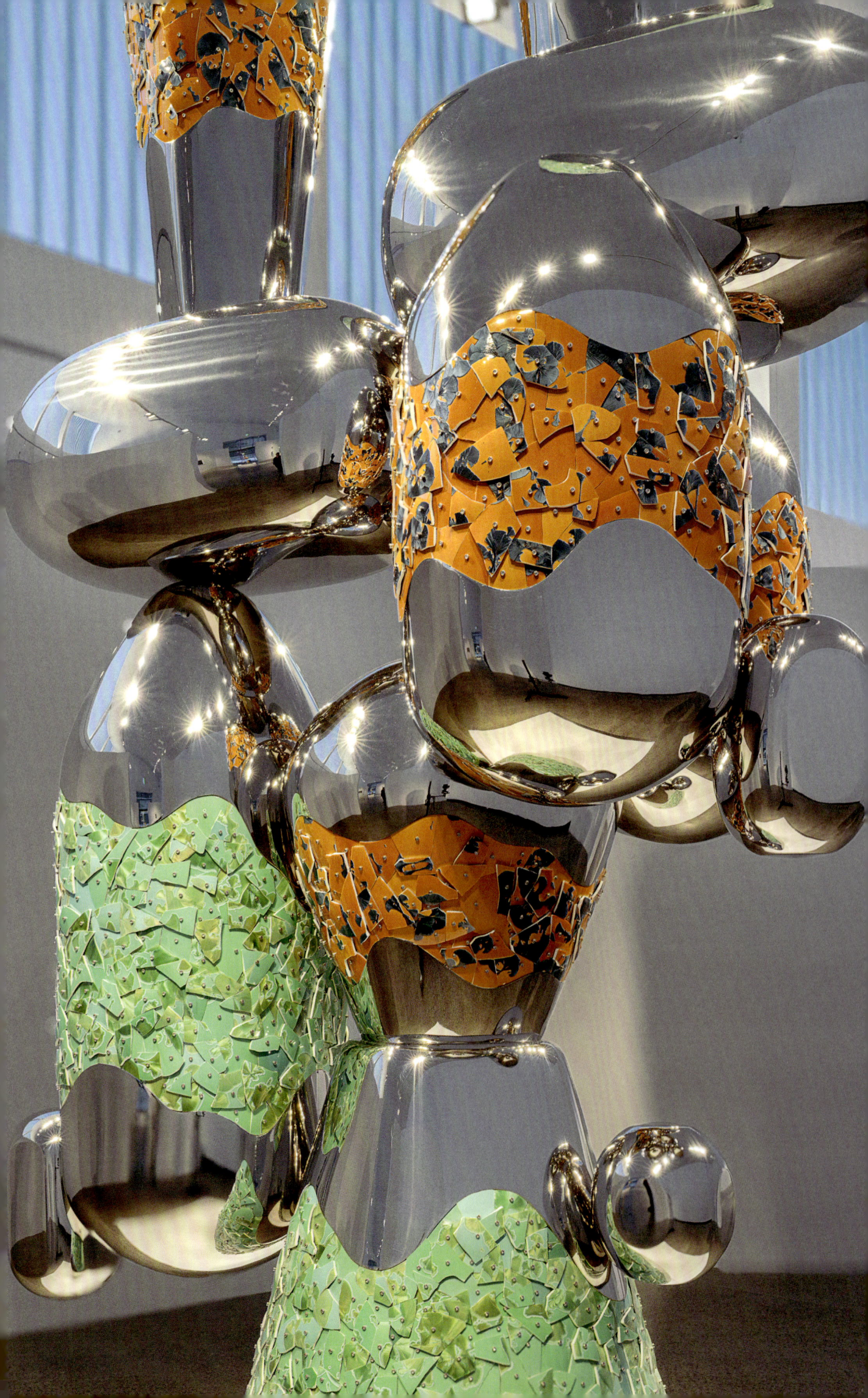

# THE PHENOMENOLOGY OF GRAVITY IN THE WORK OF LI HONGWEI

## BENJAMIN EVANS

To say that the theme of "duality" is at the core of Li Hongwei's elegant body of sculpture is, at best, an understatement. Here is a partial list of some of the binary oppositions at play in his work: Old vs. new, East vs. West, hand-made vs. industrial, delicate vs. strong, Yin vs. Yang, functional vessel vs. non-functional sculpture, lightness vs. weight, organic vs. geometric, literal vs. metaphorical, complexity vs. simplicity, the real vs. the reflection, heaven vs. earth, colorful vs. colorless, material vs. conceptual, intention vs. chance, creation vs. destruction, the perfect vs. the failure, the fragment vs. the whole—the reader is encouraged to add to this list at will.

Yet the possible interpretations of these binaries are very fluid and do not line up in any straightforward manner. The steel elements might be read as "western" owing to their association with skyscrapers, railroads and gleaming American cars, yet steel is also the fundamental building material of China's own explosive growth as an industrial superpower. The ceramic elements reference the ancient tradition of Chinese porcelain production, yet are undeniably contemporary sculpture. Clay, traditionally associated with the earth, is here often transformed into something lighter than air. Creating a simple chart of these binary oppositions is impossible.

*Li Hongwei,* Beyond the Height #5, *2024, porcelain, stainless steel, 60 x 43 x 138 inches.*

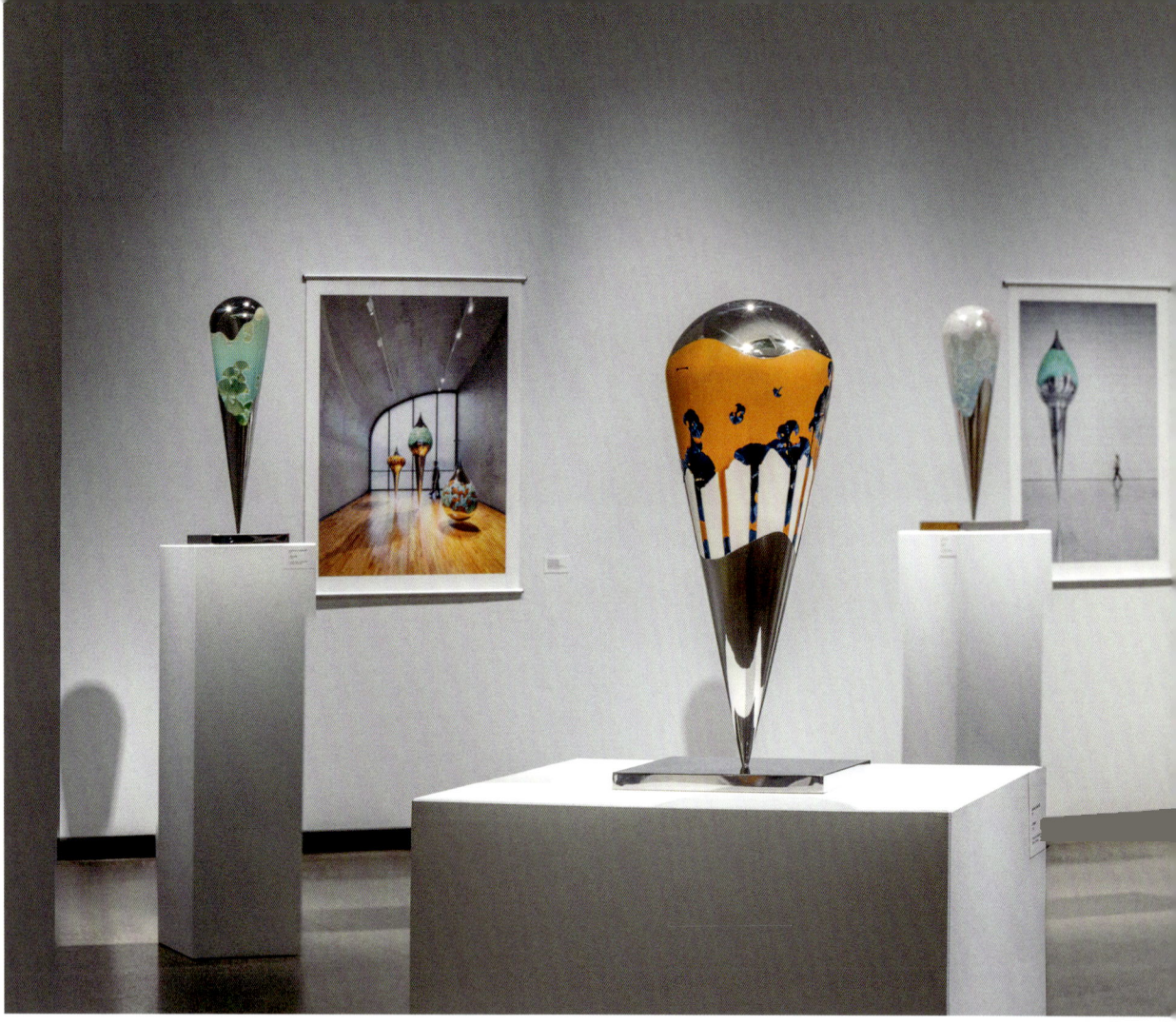

Constructing Radiance: Sculpture by Li Hongwei, *Gallery View, 2025*.

Instead, we are faced with overlapping, contradicting, and intersecting lines of interpretive possibility, something perhaps like the twigs of a bird's nest, that belie the simplicity and intuitive harmony radiating from the objects on first encounter.

This is not to say that harmony is not a central theme at stake here. In the ever-increasing articles on Li's work, virtually every commentator describes at some length the way in which he unifies these various opposing forces in line with classical Chinese aesthetic ambitions of balance and harmony. There is surely good reason for this, and these commentators are surely correct. When encountering the *Upwelling of Gravity* series, for example, the immediate experience is largely one of marvel at the harmonious, seamless blending of the contrasting materials. Achieving harmony is unquestionably a deliberate goal of the artist's process. Yet at the same time, I would like to suggest that underlying this initial sense of harmony there is also considerable tension, perhaps even conflict, lurking under the perfectly smooth, ripple-free surface. Harmony, I want to suggest, is only the starting point of an encounter with this work.

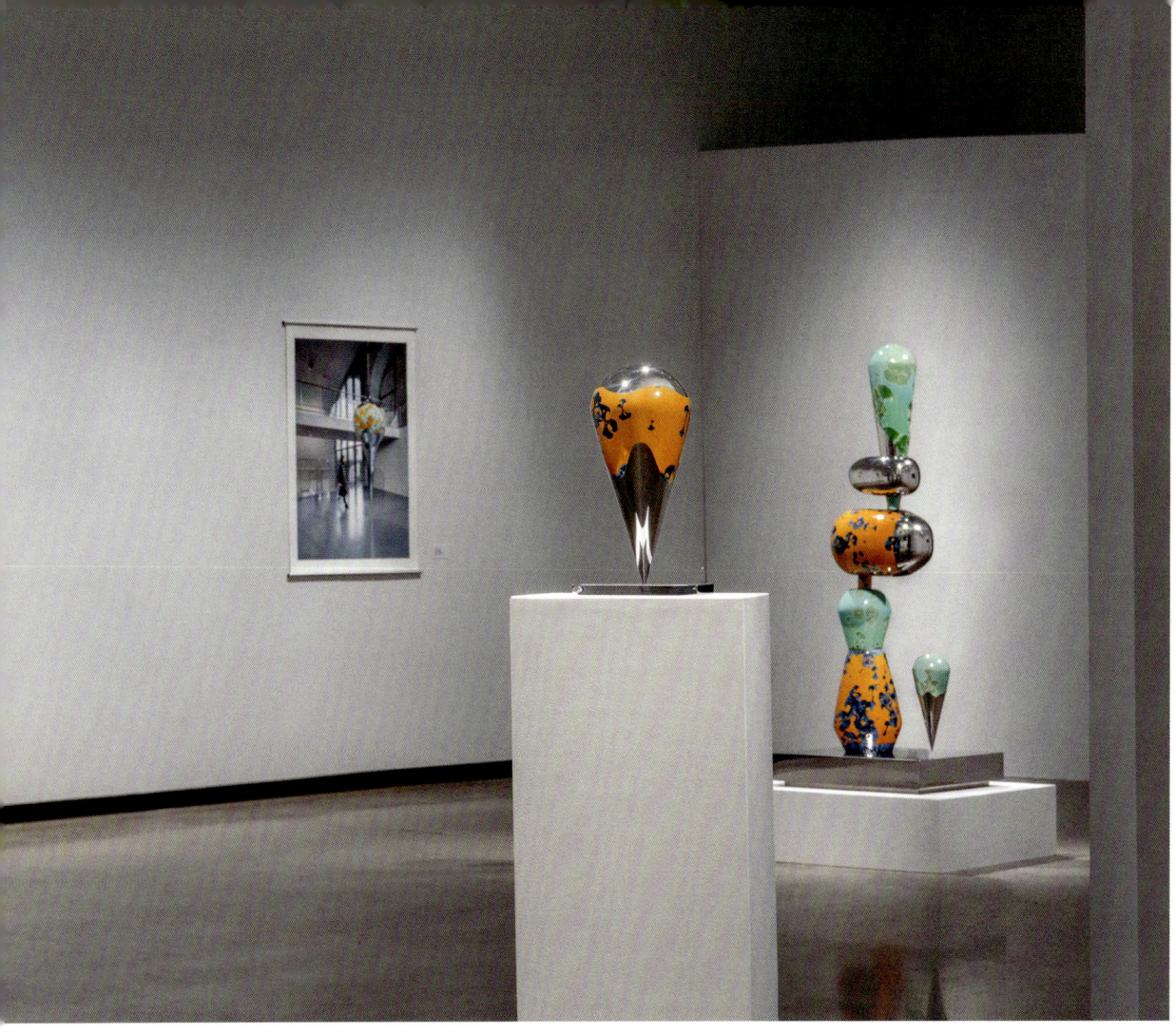

Such tension can be discovered through a simple "phenomenological" process of reflecting carefully on one's conscious experience as one moves through the exhibition. To continue with the *Upwelling of Gravity* series, moving among these works I experience, if I pay attention, a subtle but discernible shift in gravitational forces as these objects solemnly struggle to free themselves from their bases and float into the air that seems, paradoxically, to be their native environment. The smooth, circular, ceramic dome actively lifts against the square point of steel that roots it to the earth. The ceramic object, now ethereal and light, and with its references to centuries of Chinese history and tradition, is perhaps being slowly engulfed by modern metal, or at the very least being held in place, frozen. None of this is by accident. Li has repeatedly described the way in which these works are allegories of Chinese cosmology, a circular dome representing the heavens paired with a perfect square at the base, representing the earth. In this unusual arrangement, clay has become the airy dome of the Cosmos, while steel takes the place of clay to become the ordered square of Earth. The initial formal harmony of these works is undeniable, but so too is the presence of a certain tension and stress.

Likewise, the *Allegory of Balance* (Fig. 1) series suggests a very careful selection and placement process, aiming to find a harmonious wedding of multiple elements. Hybrid forms of porcelain and steel take on the appearance of mountaintop cairns, guideposts calling to mind the improbable natural stacked sculptures of Andy Goldsworthy. As in that body of work, here too there is a powerful sense of precariousness. These stacks present themselves as deliberately delicate, unbolted, unwelded, unglued together. In their proximity, museum docents must nervously stand vigilant against the exploratory palms of unattended young children, or perhaps even a poorly timed sneeze. Even the sculptures in the more solid *Dan* series, resembling so many giant eggs, appear not merely placed but rather *poised* on an invisible edge, awaiting only a misdirected breath to come crashing down. Observing exhibition visitors I have on more than one occasion seen a tempted hand reaching out to see whether or not the forms are as mobile as they appear (which indeed they are).

The source of these tensions, at least those I've described so far, is unambiguous: simple physics. Gravity, as unrelenting as it is mysterious, pulls on the sculpted forms even as Li attempts to play with it. In *Xuan #30*, a lodestone dangles precariously from a thin cable, which in context reads like a thread from some mechanical spider. In *Allegory of Balance #41*, a conical form likewise hangs mere millimeters from the base. In direct contrast with the figures in the Upwelling series, here the objects, whose elegant steel bases are honed to an almost fragile pin-point, are aiming at the floor, and even a viewer disinclined to phenomenology can't help but feel the pull of gravity as they approach. As with the eggs of the *Dan* series, these pendulums remain motionless, but here the motionlessness becomes palpable because of the possibility of motion, the stillness itself creating its own tangible presence. By drawing us into the invisible physical forces at play around us, Li in fact begins to gently guide us beyond the physical. Far from harmonious, here the physical moves into tension with the metaphysical, the spiritual heights to which Li ambitiously hopes to direct our attention.

Nowhere is this more evident than the monumental masterpiece *Beyond the Height #5*. Inspired only in part by the physical forms of the great Cereus cacti of the Arizona desert, Li's interest was in the psychological or even spiritual experience he had when encountering them for the first time, and it is this phenomenological aspect he is trying to capture through the interplay of dualisms contained in the work. Compared to the smaller works of the *Allegory of Balance* series, here the towering pile of gleaming objects has a much more solid and grounded feel. There is no longer any danger that it will all collapse at any moment. On the contrary, after our initial glance to its heights, we are confident

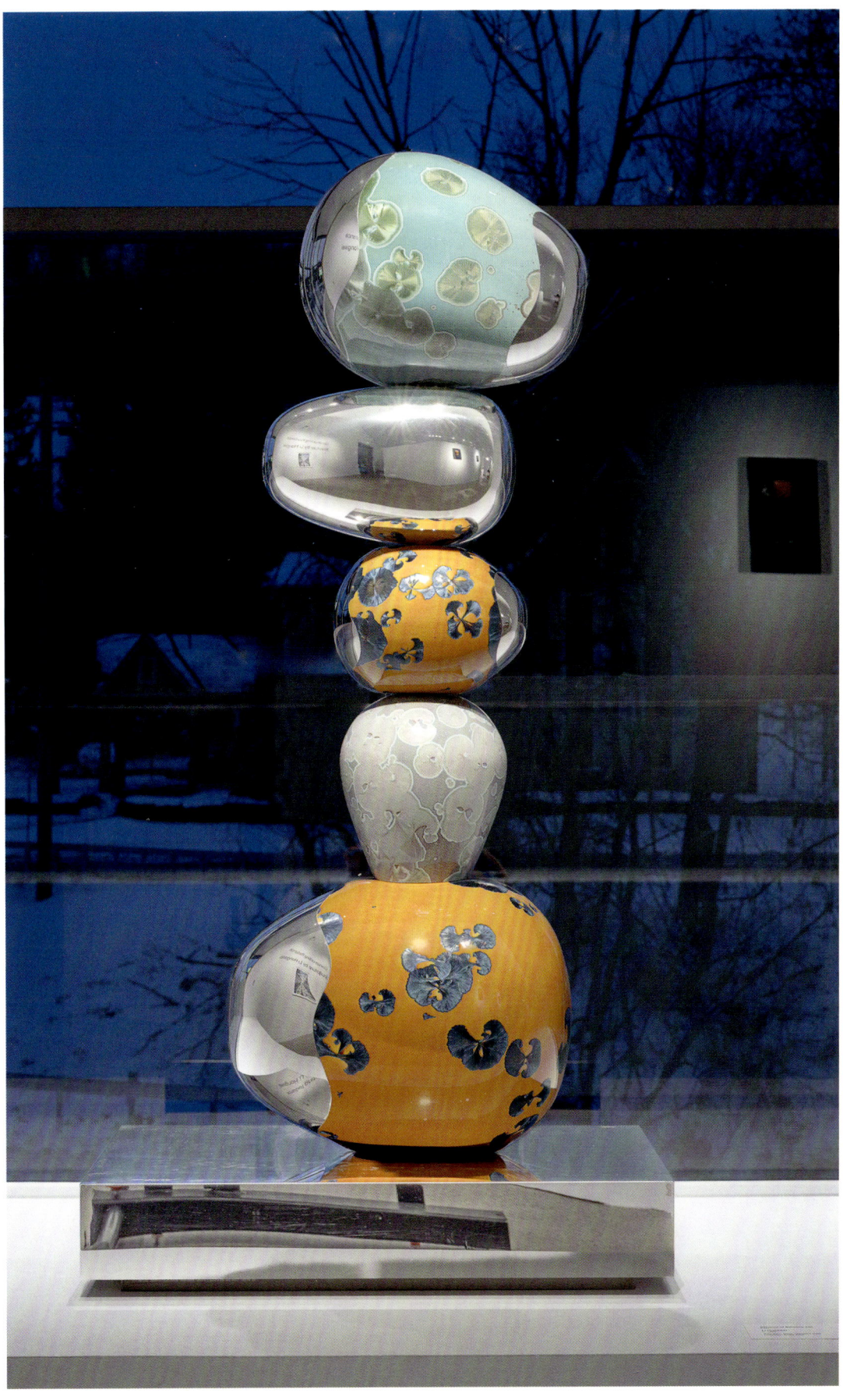

*Fig. 1:* *Li Hongwei,* Allegory of Balance #40, *2024, porcelain, stainless steel, 26 x 18 x 50 inches.*

enough to be drawn in to investigate the fragments of colored ceramic bolted firmly around the perimeters of various steel bodies. As the realization dawns that these fragments are from the very same vessels on display at the entrance to the show, we are pulled in closer still to investigate the precise miniature screw heads, which might call to mind (for those of a certain imaginative bent) the rivets on the armor of the thousands of buried terracotta warriors in Xi'an. (Fig. 2) Even the unorthodox screws themselves demand attention, with thick cylindrical heads and hexagonal fittings. Unlike the other works in the show, which almost seem to have appeared effortlessly *ex nihilo*, here we become much more aware that what we are experiencing has been deliberately constructed into exactly this form. Stepping back now, the eye is caught by its own reflection in the steel surface, which at this scale functions as a full-length mirror. We are trapped on the deep surface of the work, looking at a version of ourselves looking back from the inside. We might become aware of others around us, sharing the experience, or, if alone, of the empty space of the gallery appearing inside the sculpture itself. Inside and outside, one of the most primitive of dualisms, are momentarily reversed and we are disoriented, unsure. Perhaps we take a step back again now, hesitating before the complicated forces at play around us. Again we look up, but this time not with a glance, now with a deliberate gaze, as if standing before a sacred monolith in an alien temple, which, in a certain sense, is exactly what we are doing. Again, there is harmony here, but also a disquieting uneasiness, the tension one feels in the face of things we do not understand.

Immanuel Kant, arguably the most important German philosopher of all time, had a name for this, or for something relevantly similar, which might help to articulate what seems to be going on here. Kant, who adored philosophical jargon, came up with the phrase "the antimonies of experience" to name contradictions that necessarily arise when the limited human mind attempts to step beyond the scope of its powers. The mind, for example, takes up two quite natural, plausible thoughts like "all things must have a beginning" and "the universe is infinite, with no beginning or end," and runs into stark and unresolvable contradiction. This demonstrated quite concretely, for Kant at least, the limits of human understanding, and the need to articulate human knowledge as bound by certain limits. Whether Kant's notion of antimonies function philosophically as he wanted them to (consensus seems to be that they don't), I think Li's "antimonies" are working perfectly. The contradictions of the forever multiplying dualities, the harmonies, resonances, and tensions formed between them create in the viewer a kind of rupture, deliberately revealing the limits of our understanding of the physical world, but in so doing directing our attention to a place beyond physics, beyond gravity, beyond dimension, "beyond the height." From physics we are, again, lead inexorably to metaphysics.

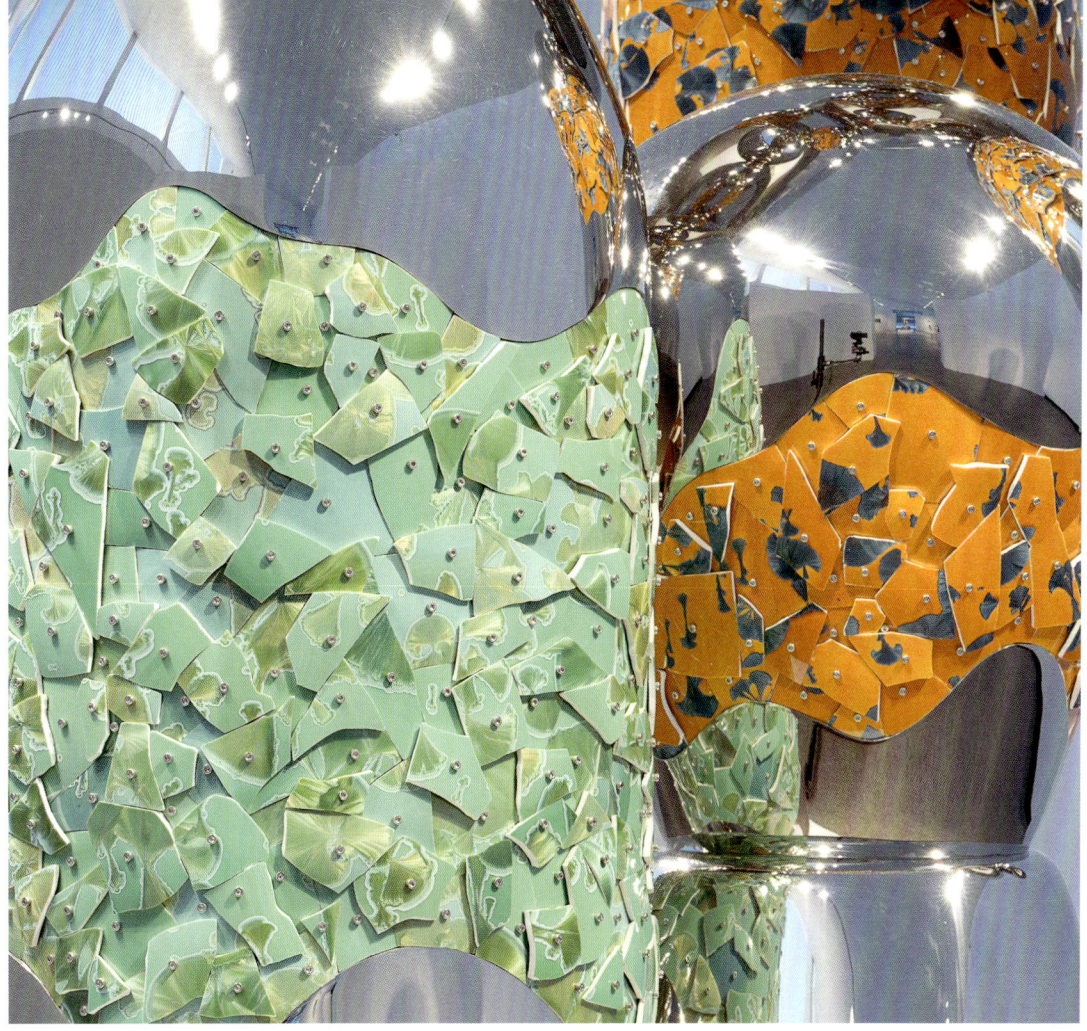

*Fig. 2: detail: Li Hongwei,* Beyond the Height #5*, 2024, porcelain, stainless steel*
*60 x 43 x 138 inches.*

To return from these heights of philosophy I would like to call attention to one final moment of tension and dualism unique to this particular exhibition of Li Hongwei's oeuvre, that of Work vs. Play. For surely one access point into this body of work is through the door of playfulness, through his joyful experimentation with materiality as such. In conversation, Li has explained that he aspires to have his work seem utterly light, effortless, like an athlete performing some impossible maneuver while making it look easy. It is worth stating clearly at this point that Li is completely involved in every single part of his production process. He builds the vessels, manages the complicated firing the crystalline glaze demands, shatters the pots deemed imperfect, sketches the imagined sculptures, works out the engineering, builds models, carves Styrofoam, casts, molds, and polishes huge quantities of steel, and when required, hand screws thousands of fragments together to create his final result. This list alone puts paid to the idea that the work is easy or effortless, yet this effort is never made visible to the viewer. "Constructing Radiance" is the first exhibition in which the public has had the opportunity to catch a few small glimpses behind the wizard's curtain, in the form of a handful of photographs from his studio and preliminary sketches for his work.

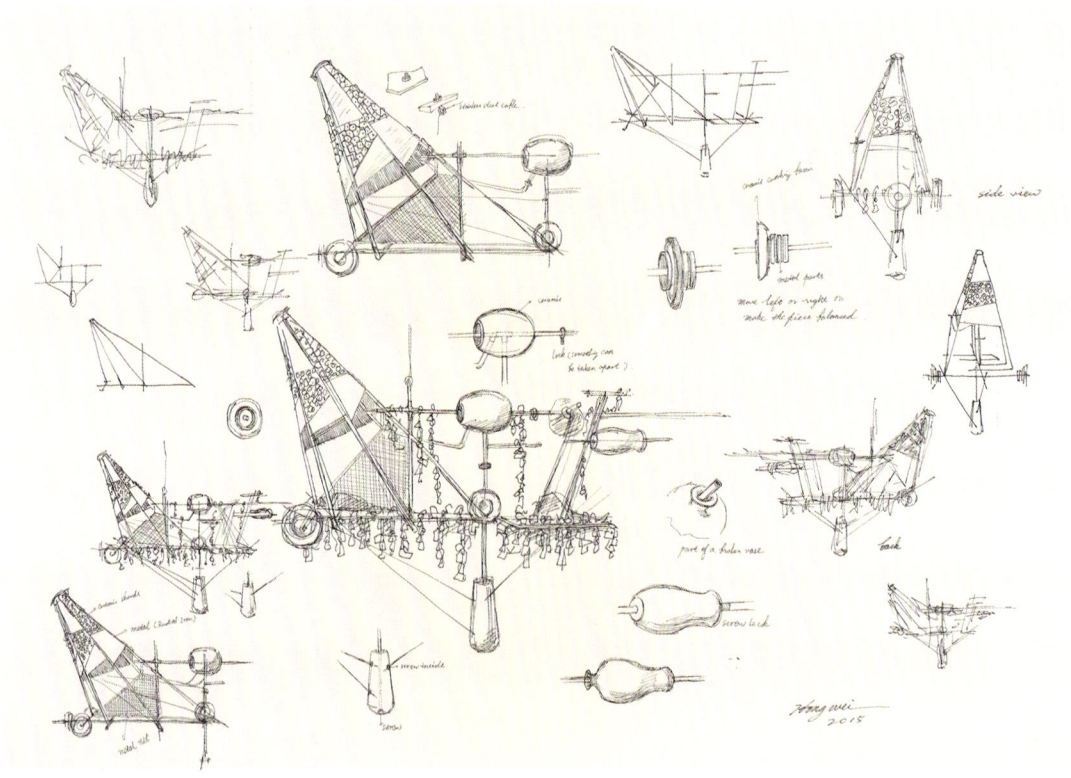

*Fig. 3: Li Hongwei,* Rebirth in Breakage, *working drawing, ink on paper, 31.25 x 21.5 Inches.*

In the drawings (Fig. 3) we can see Li repeatedly sketching on page after page the same mechanisms which compose *Rebirth in Breakage*, as though caught in the grip of an undiagnosed obsessive compulsion. The drawings contain no measurements, and are not intended as blueprints, but rather are what is left behind by somebody almost ritually working out a complex idea. If the drawings reveal a degree of mental labor, the photographs reveal some sense of the manual labor involved Hongwei's work. In one, Li squats behind a field of pot shards, surrounded by nearly perfect vessels of many colors, holding a large hammer and looking stoically, even defiantly at the camera (Fig. 4). In my favorite, eight adult men in overalls are at work on various elements, some grinding steel, some welding behind a shower of sparks, some poised (but unposed) on scaffolding to hold unfinished sections in place. Here we see that all the seemingly effortless, easy play of Li's practice is in fact an enormous amount of work, that radiance IS in fact a construction to which he routinely devotes ten-hour days. Perhaps one of the most telling fragments of evidence for all this came to me from a brief moment during an artist talk Li gave as part of the exhibition program. For a few seconds there appeared on the screen a photograph of the reverse sides of a vast collection of pottery shards being prepared for a monumental work, and we could see the shards were all numbered. Each shard had an exact place in the final composition, a fixed position in what appeared to be a totally chaotic jumble of things. This level of precision, of perfectionism, is unparalleled in my experience of working with contemporary artists, and activated yet another duality at stake in the work, that between order and chaos.

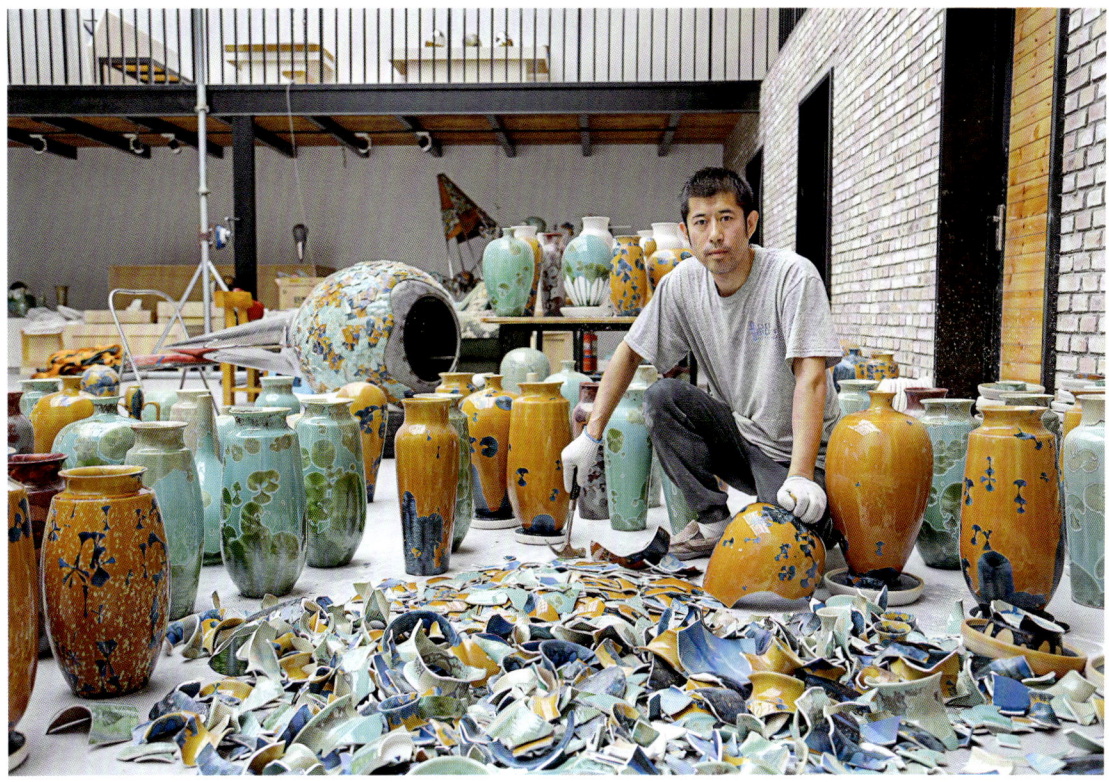

*Fig. 4: Li Hongwei, 2022, making porcelain shards. Li Hongwei studio, Beijing, China*

In traditional Anglo-American philosophy the word "dualism" is used to refer to the commonplace idea that there exist in the world two, and only two, fundamental kinds of things: the physical and the spiritual. In textbooks it is typically associated with Early Modern European thinkers like Rene Descartes, but the basic idea persists as not only the cornerstone of most religions but also the general worldview of almost three quarters of the world's population. Li Hongwei's work provides us the possibility of revisiting this pedestrian version of dualism, replacing it with multiple binaries in which physical objects lead us first to invisible physical forces and from there to possibilities beyond. It is perhaps a commonplace observation that all art, at least the most interesting, operates at the intersection of mind and world. By delicately playing with the invisible forces of the visible world, Li Hongwei's sculpture is a multi-dimensional car crash at that intersection, such that one can no longer tell where one ends and the other begins.

Benjamin Evans

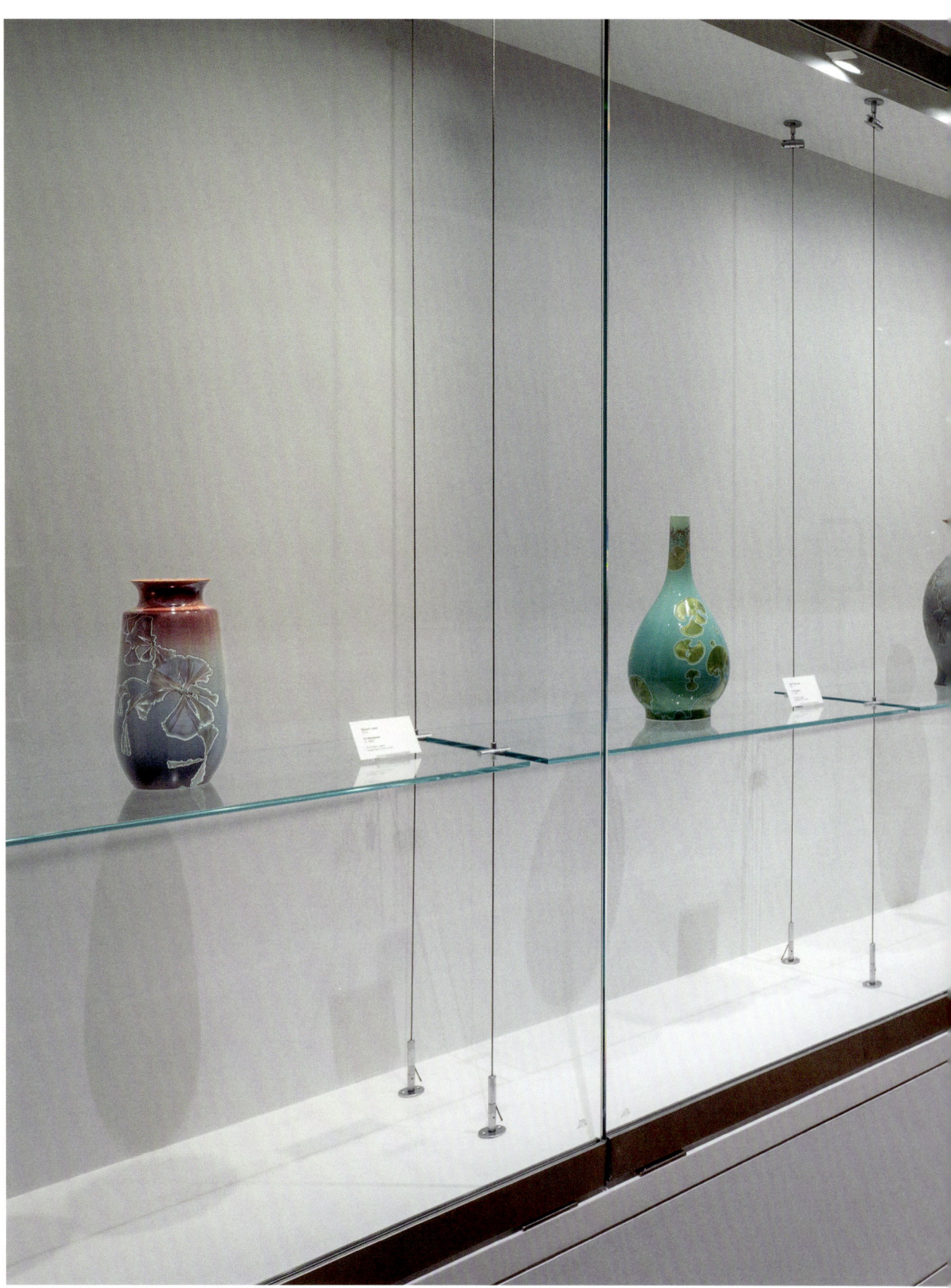

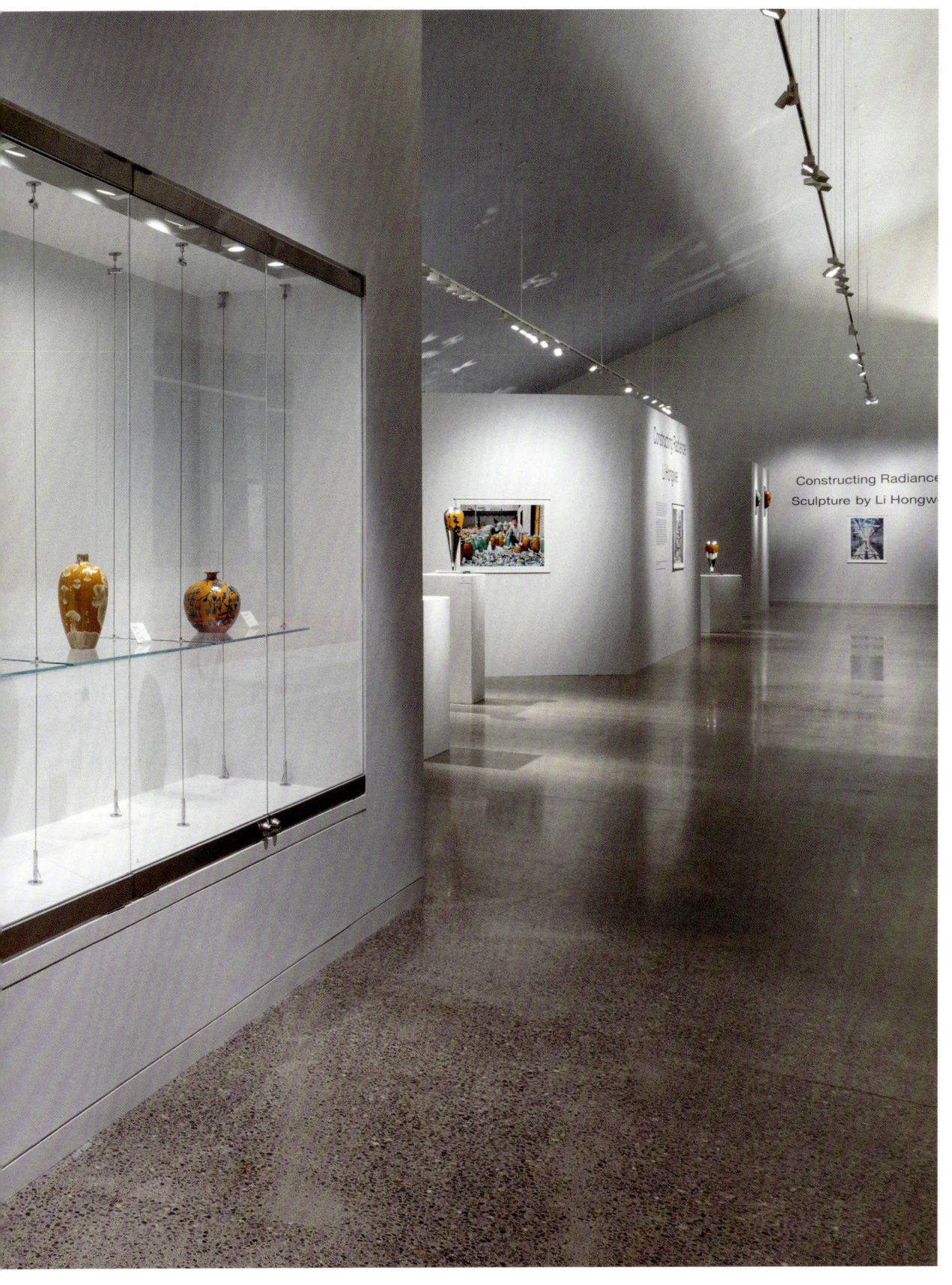

GALLERY

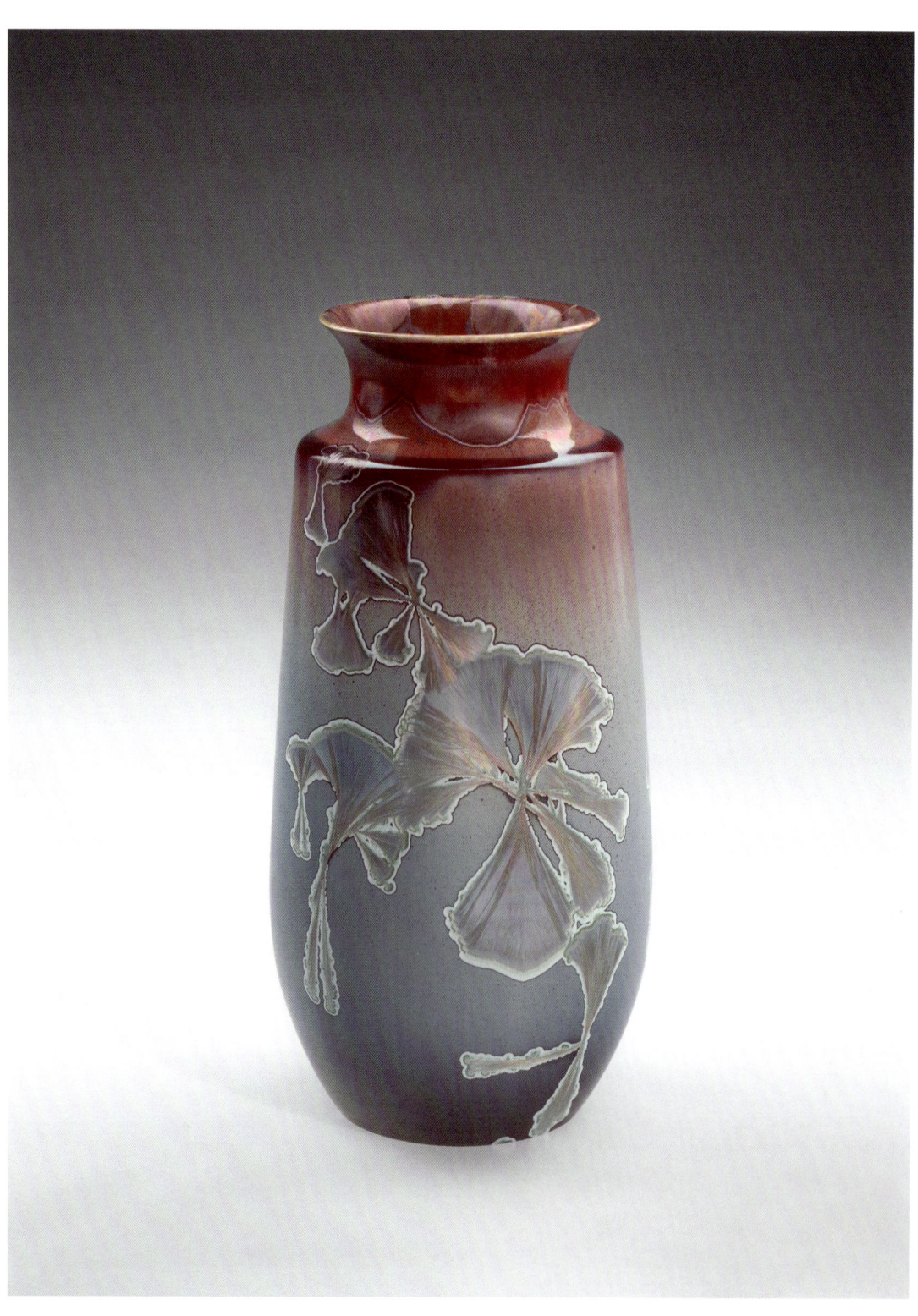

*Li Hongwei,* Gourd Vase, *2018, porcelain 5.5 x 5.5 x 11.4 inches.*

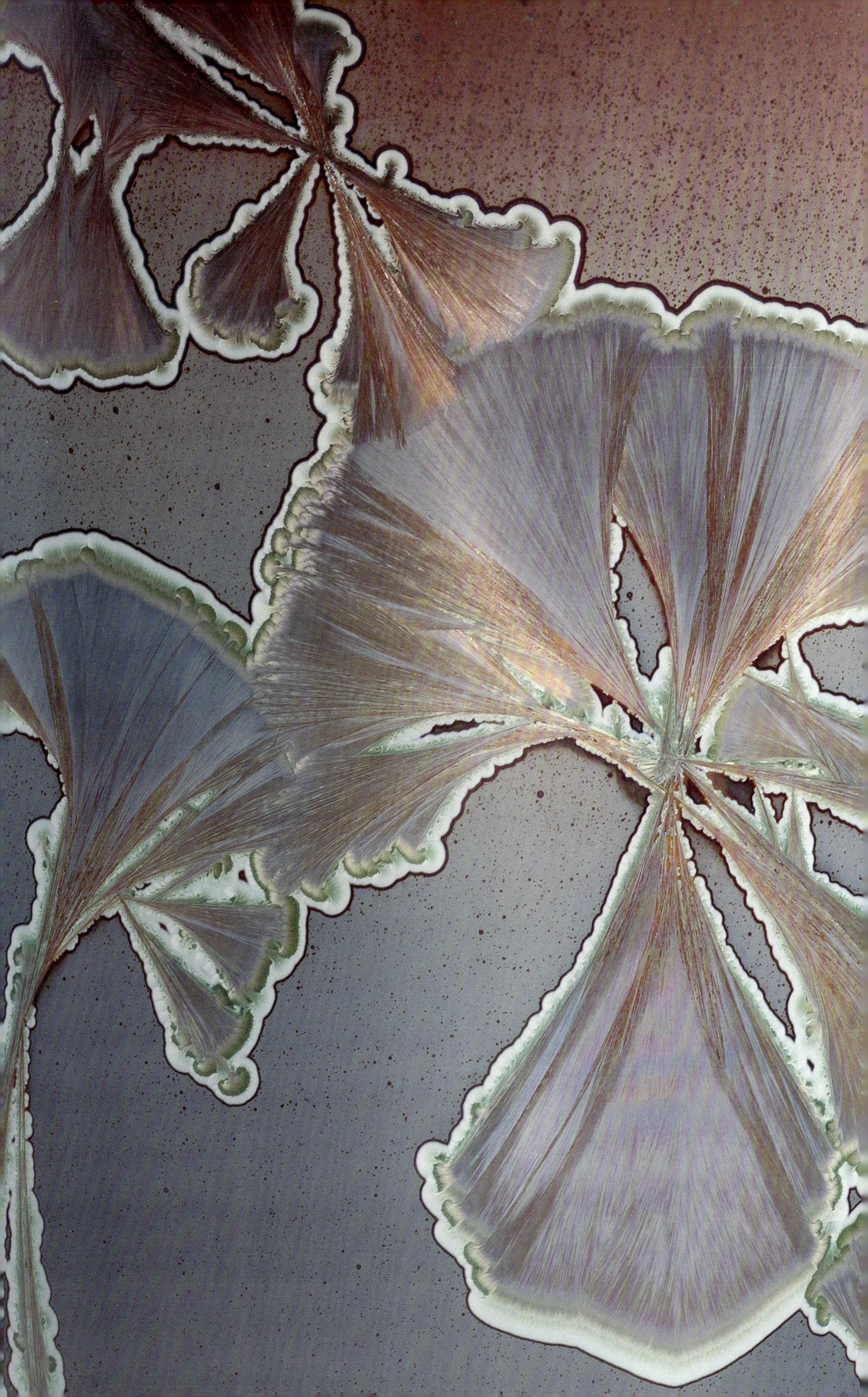

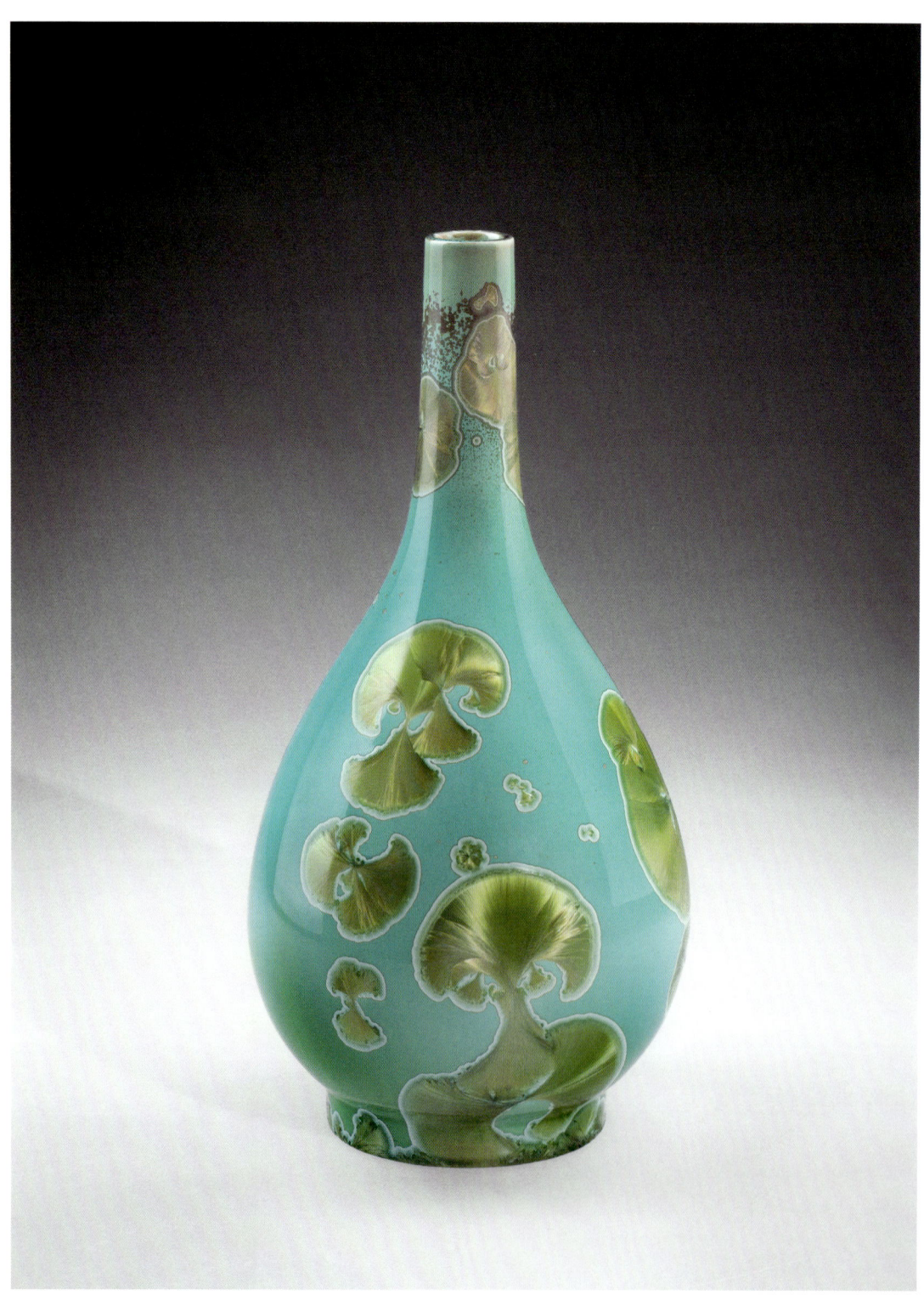

*Li Hongwei,* Dan Ping Vase*, 2023, porcelain, 8x8x16 inches.*

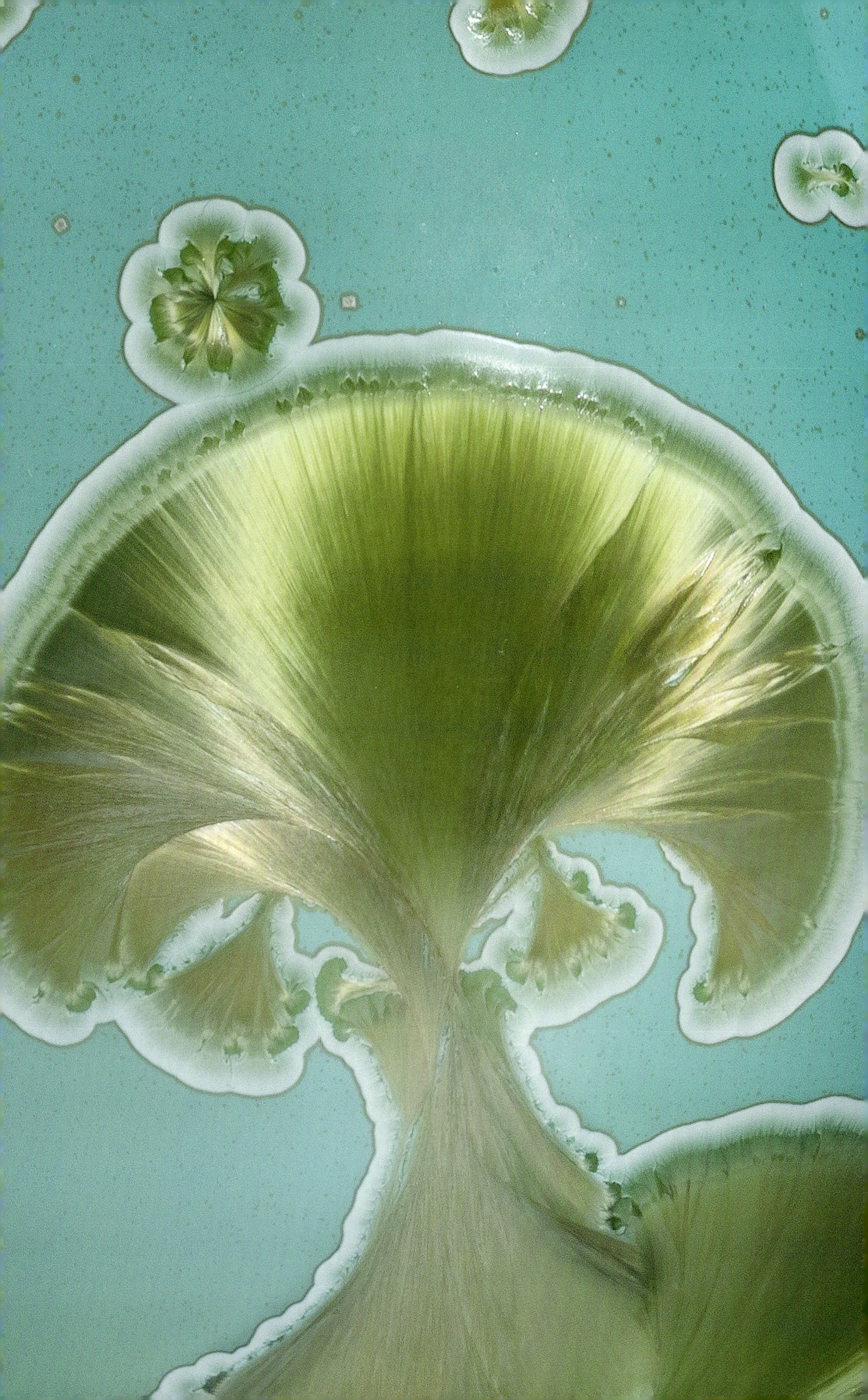

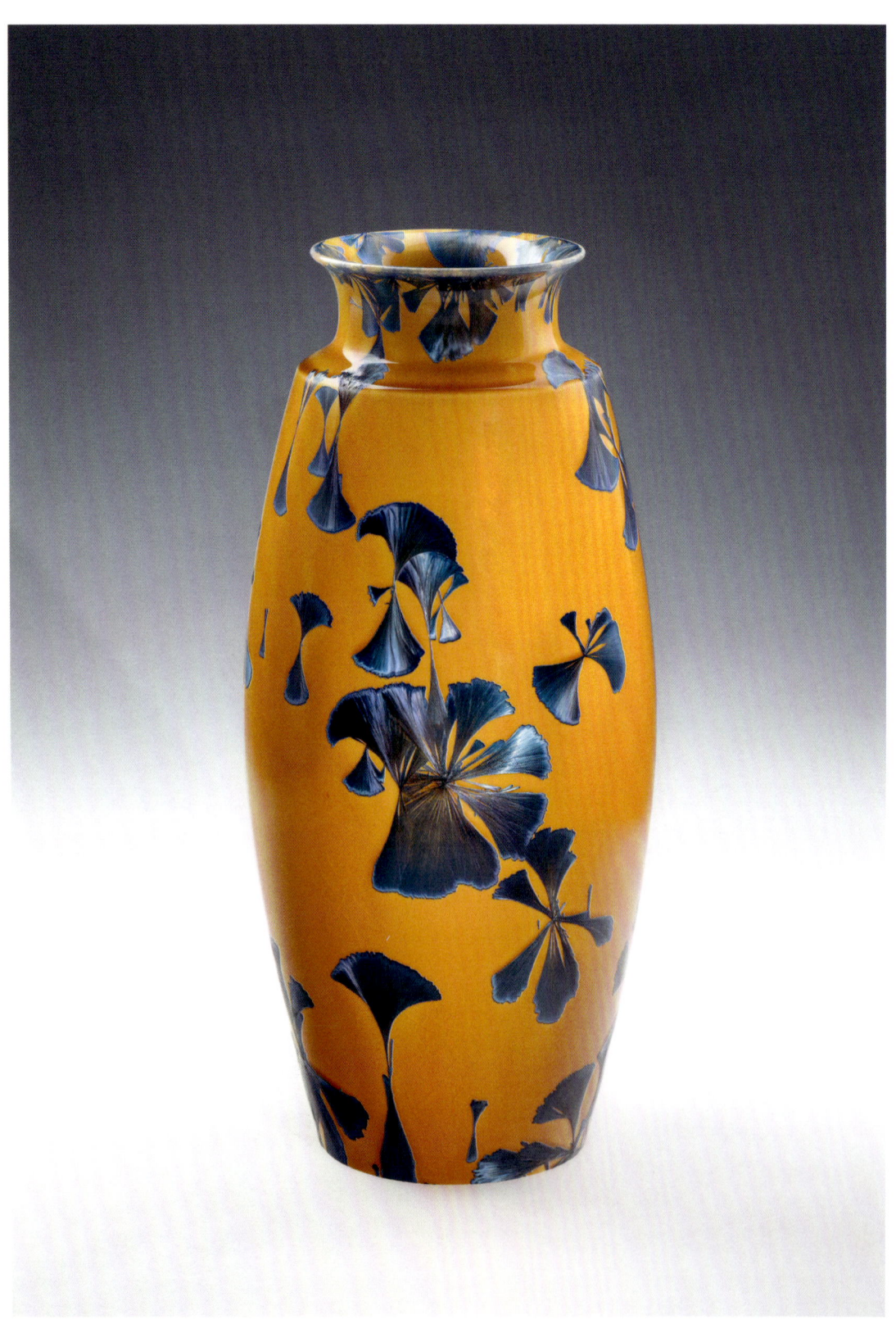

*Li Hongwei,* Drum Vase, *2022, porcelain, 7 x 7 x 15.5 inches.*

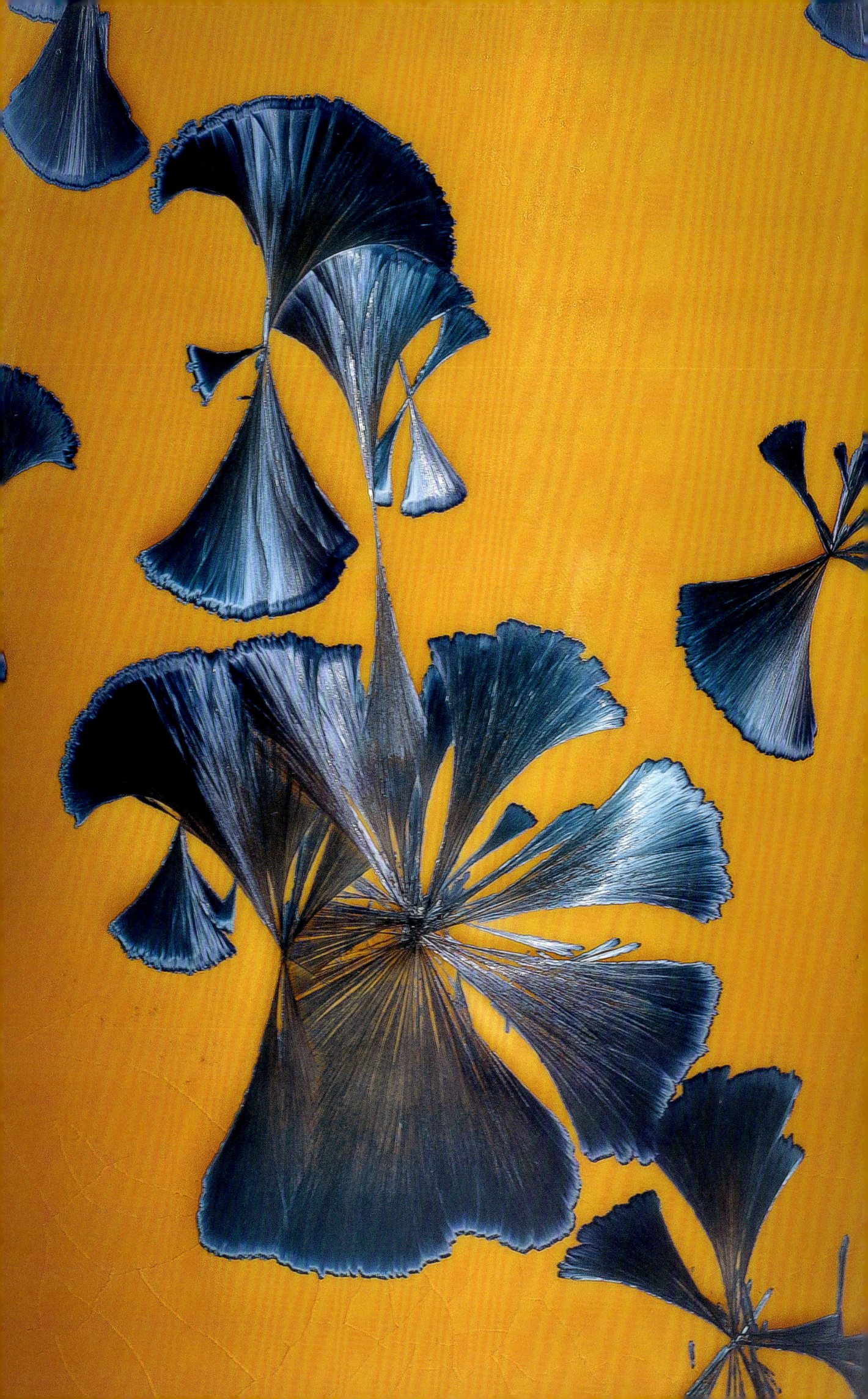

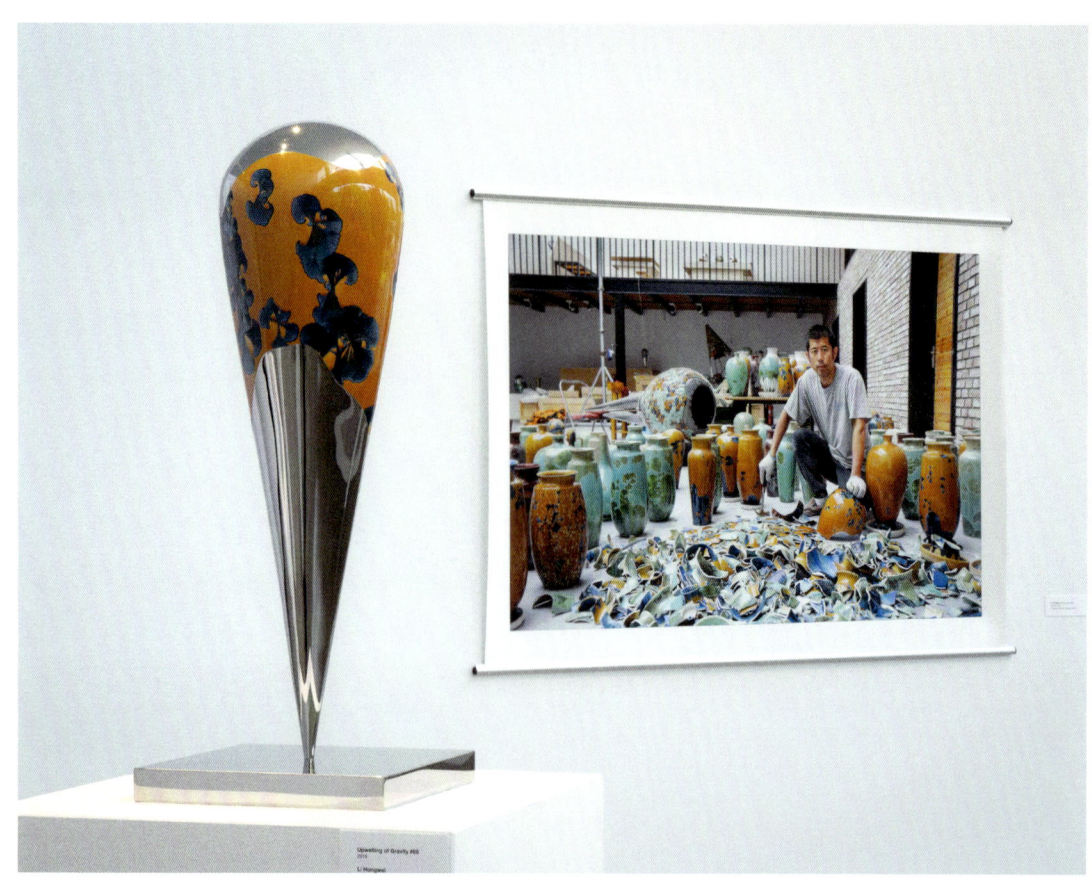

*Li Hongwei,* Upwelling of Gravity #69, *2019, porcelain, stainless steel, 9.8 x 9.8 x 24.5 inches, foreground. Li Hongwei, Beijing, 2022, background.*

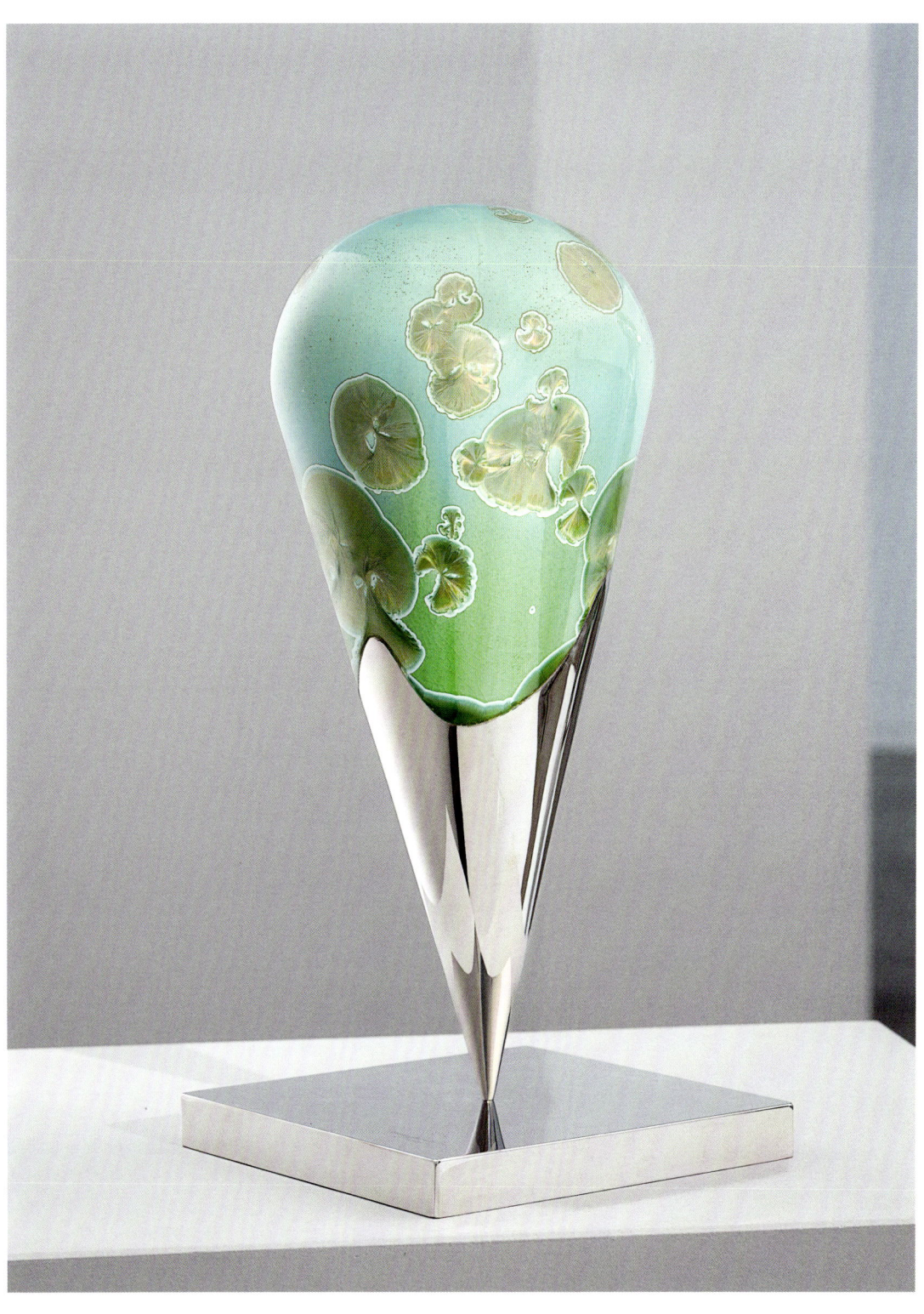

*Li Hongwei,* Upwelling of Gravity #3, *2017, porcelain, stainless steel, 9.8 x9.8 x 21 inches.*

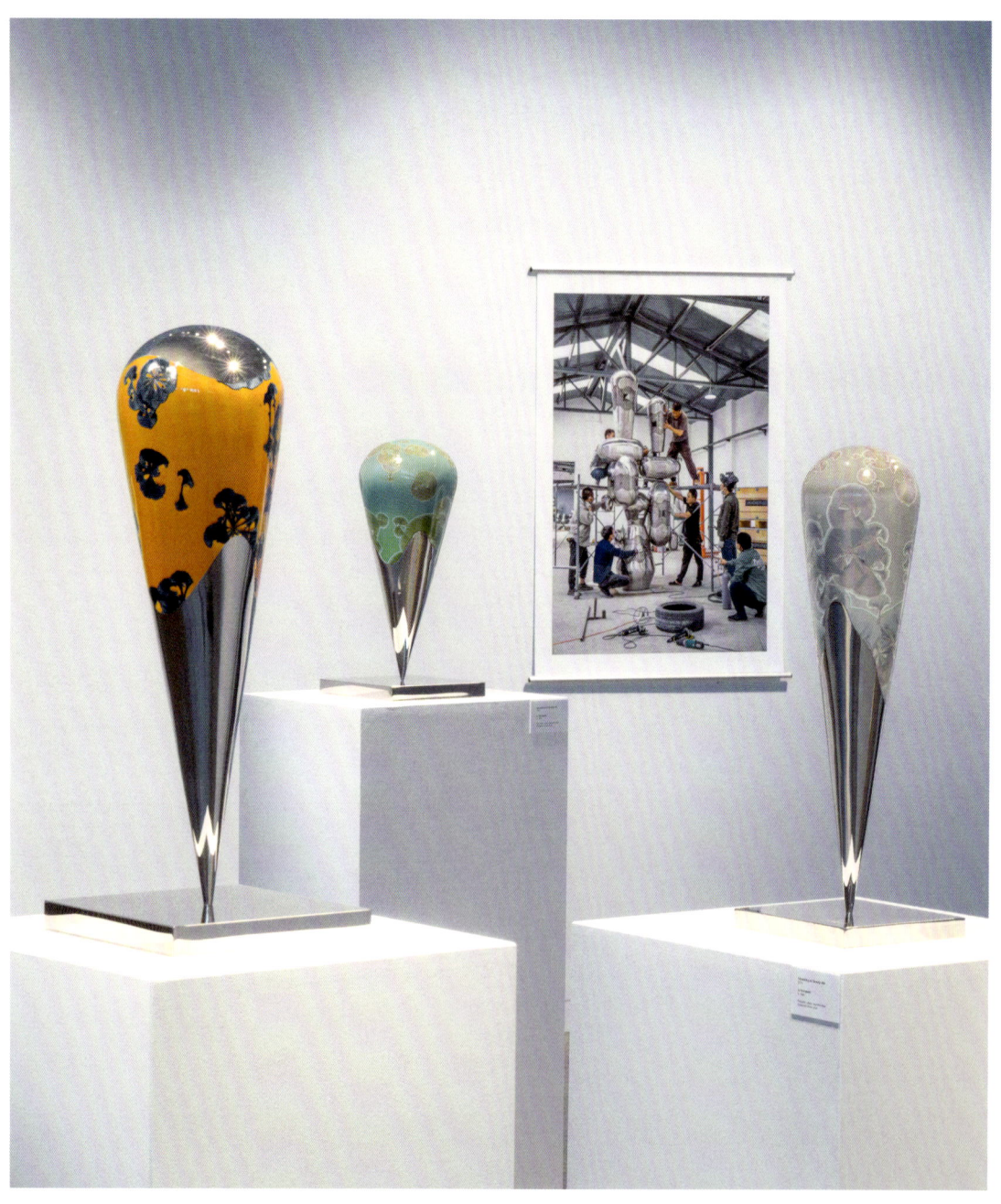

Constructing Radiance: Sculpture by Li Hongwei, *Gallery View, 2025.*

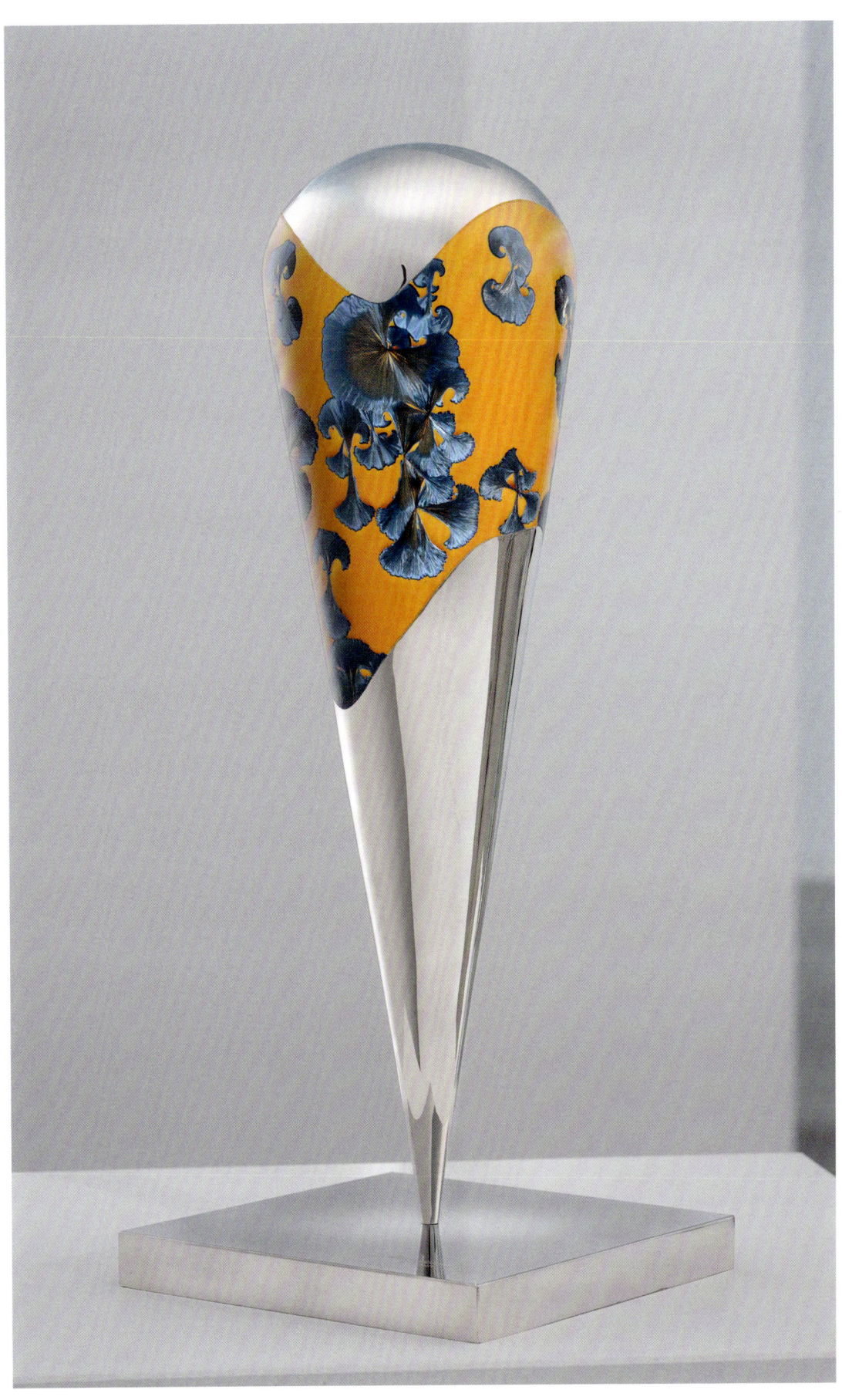

*Li Hongwei,* Upwelling of Gravity #69, *2019, porcelain, stainless steel 9.8 x 9.8 x 24.5 inches.*

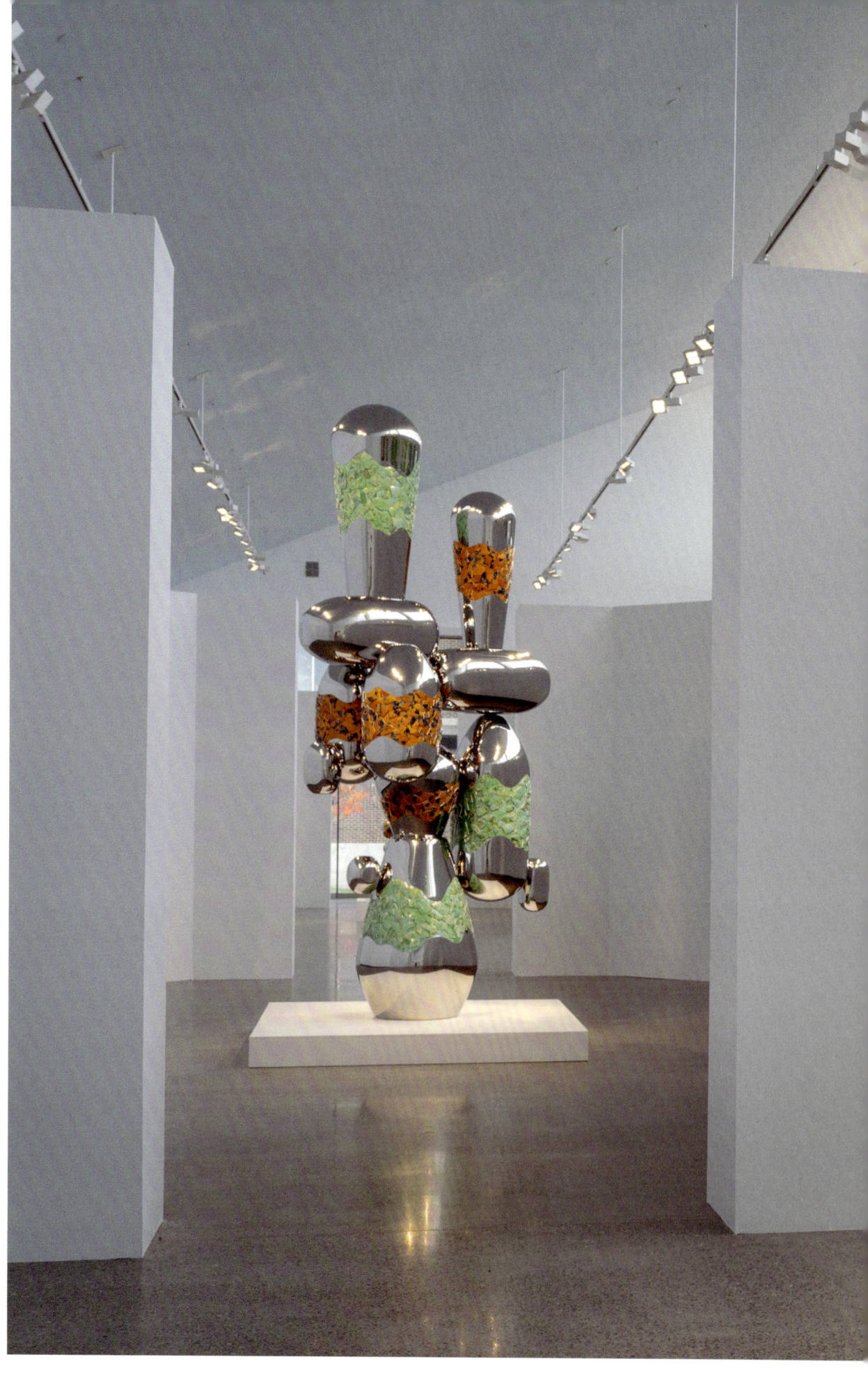

Constructing Radiance: Sculpture by Li Hongwei, *Gallery View, 2025*.

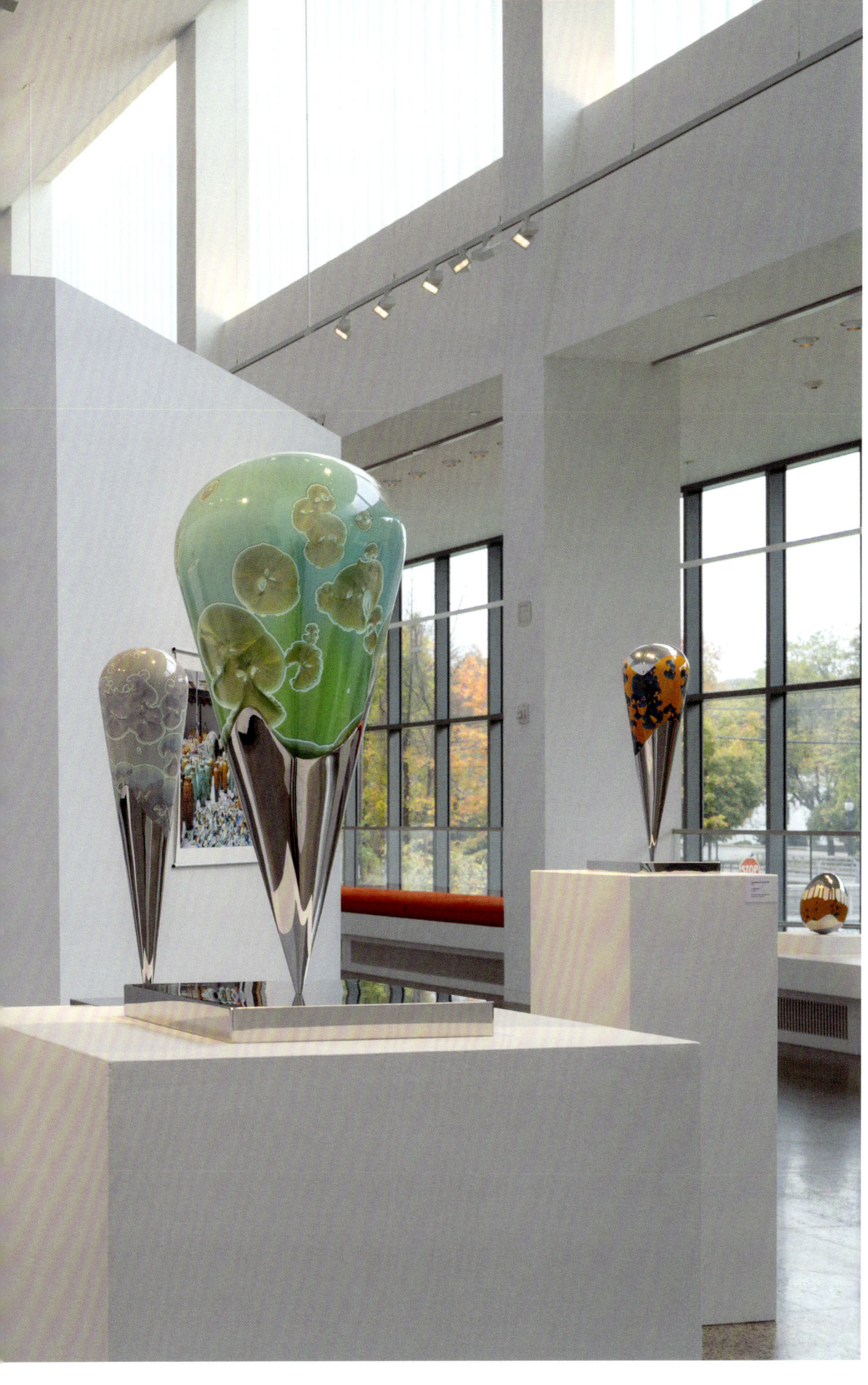

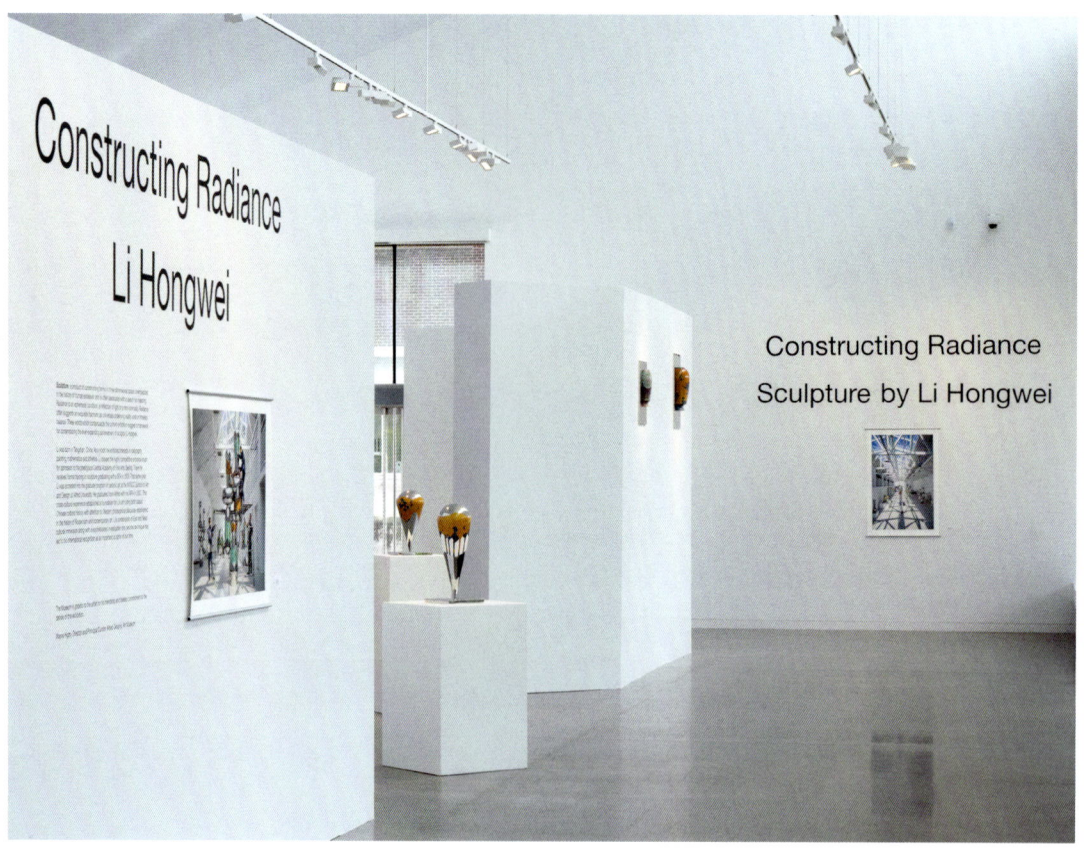

Constructing Radiance: Sculpture by Li Hongwei, *Gallery View, 2025.*

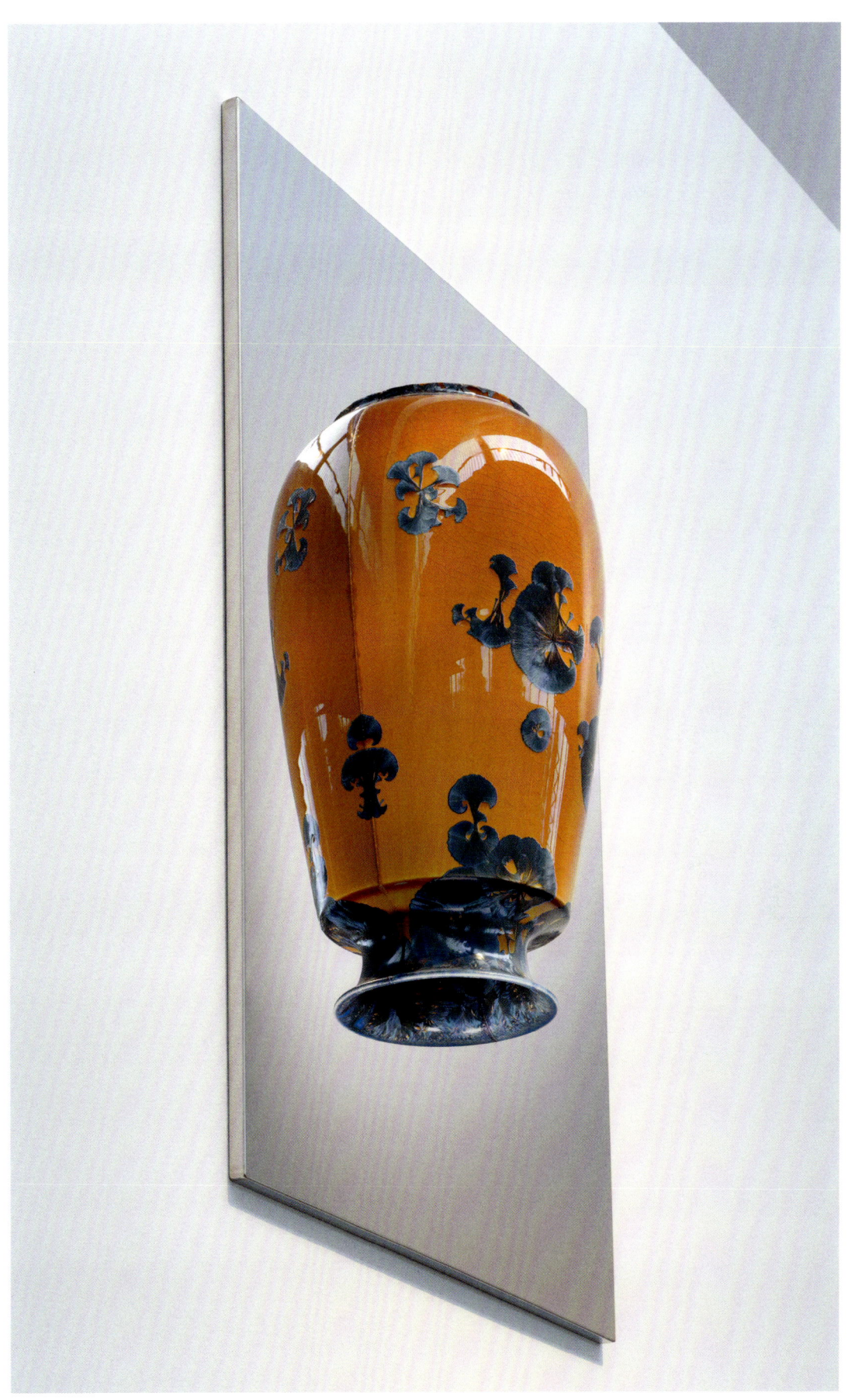

*Li Hongwei, Illusion #4, 2017, porcelain, stainless steel, 26 x 18 x 9 inches.*

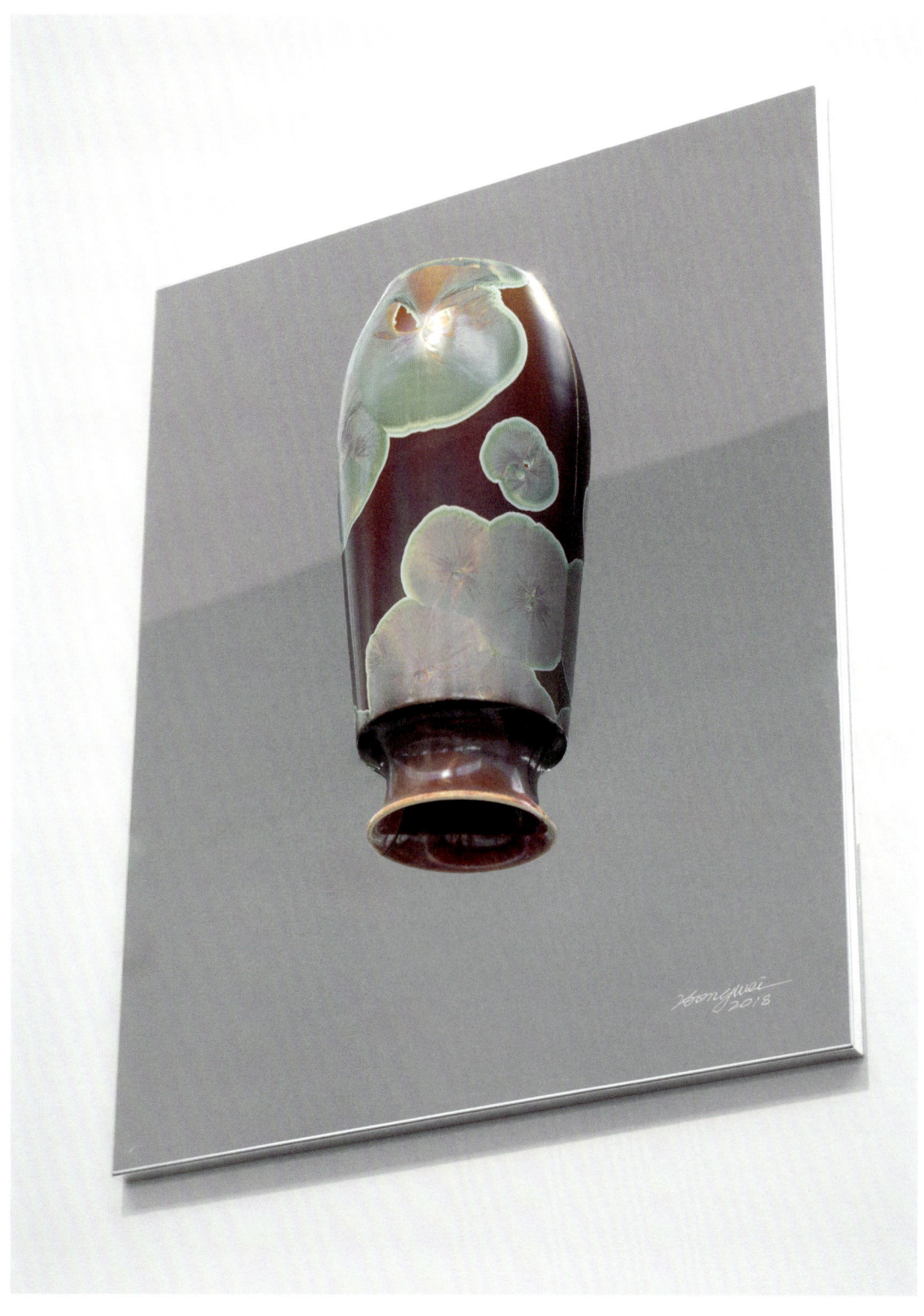

*Li Hongwei,* Illusion #9, *2019, porcelain, stainless steel, 19.7 x 15.7 x 5.1 inches.*

*Opposite Page:* Constructing Radiance: Sculpture by Li Hongwei, *Gallery View, featuring* Illusion #9 *2025.*

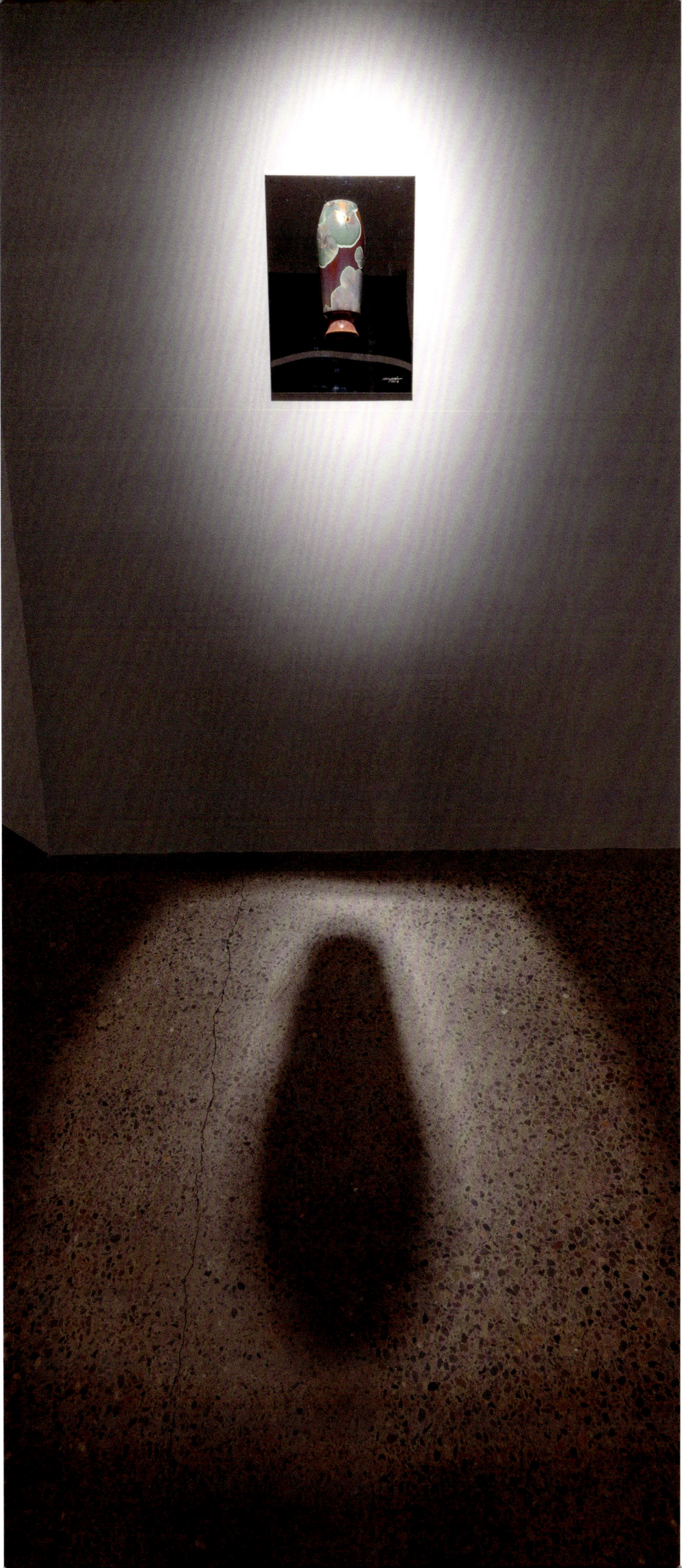

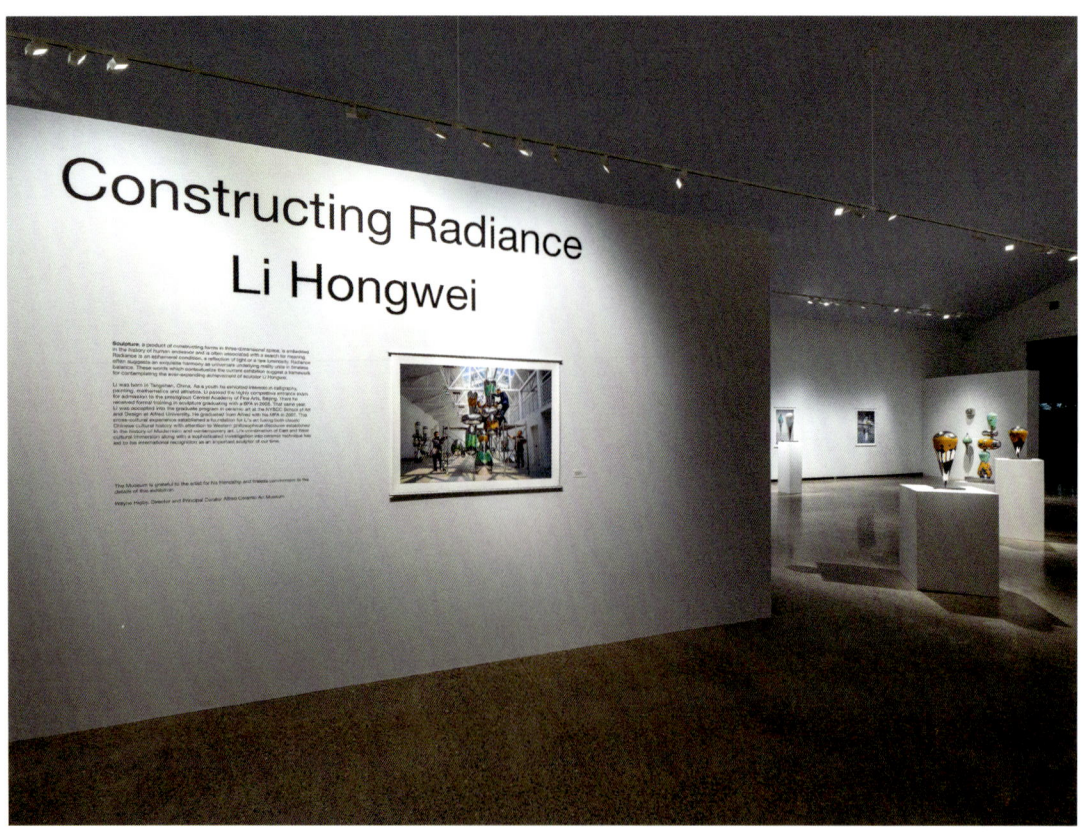

Constructing Radiance: Sculpture by Li Hongwei, *Gallery View, 2025.*

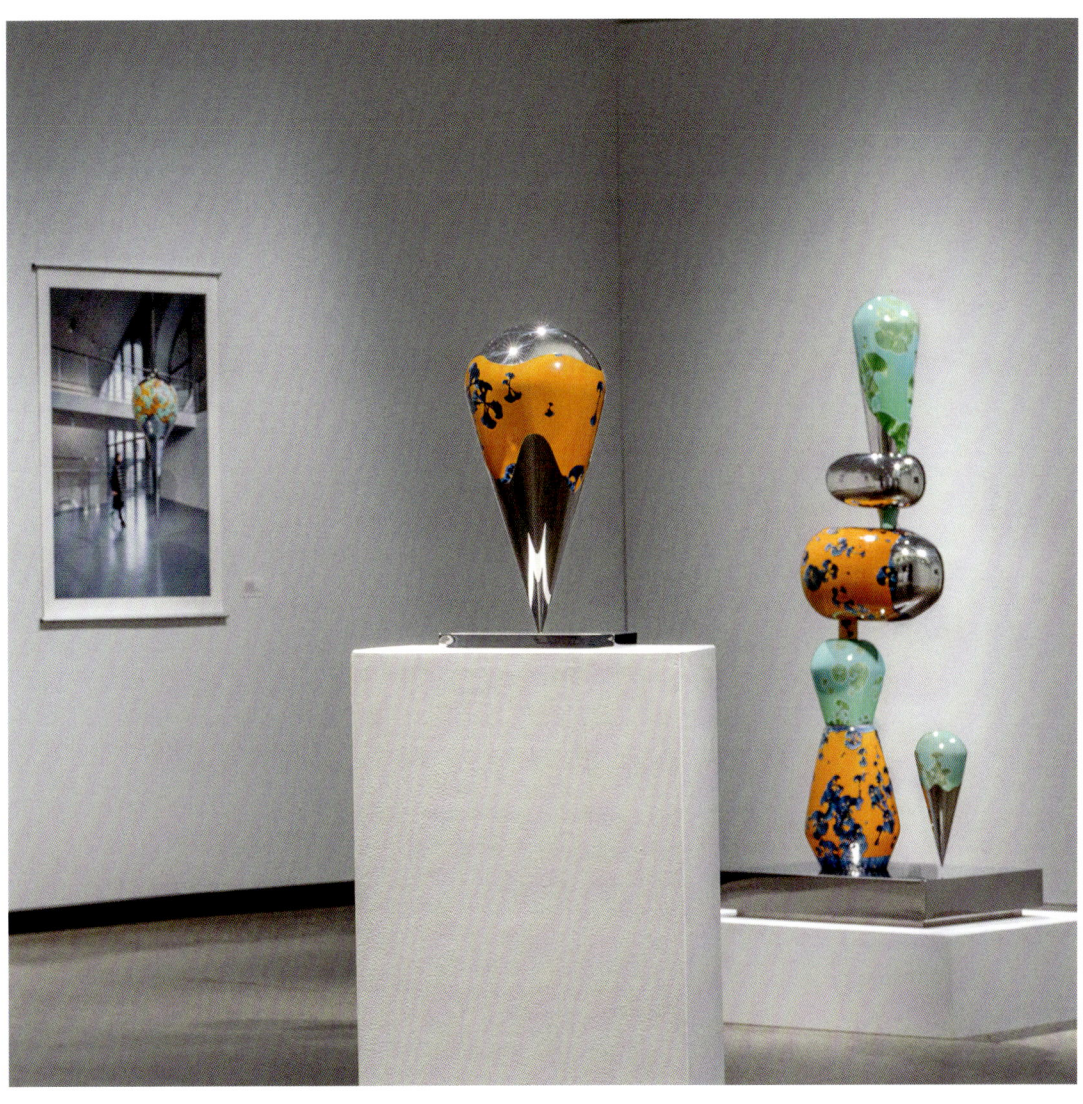

Constructing Radiance: Sculpture by Li Hongwei, *Gallery View, 2025*.

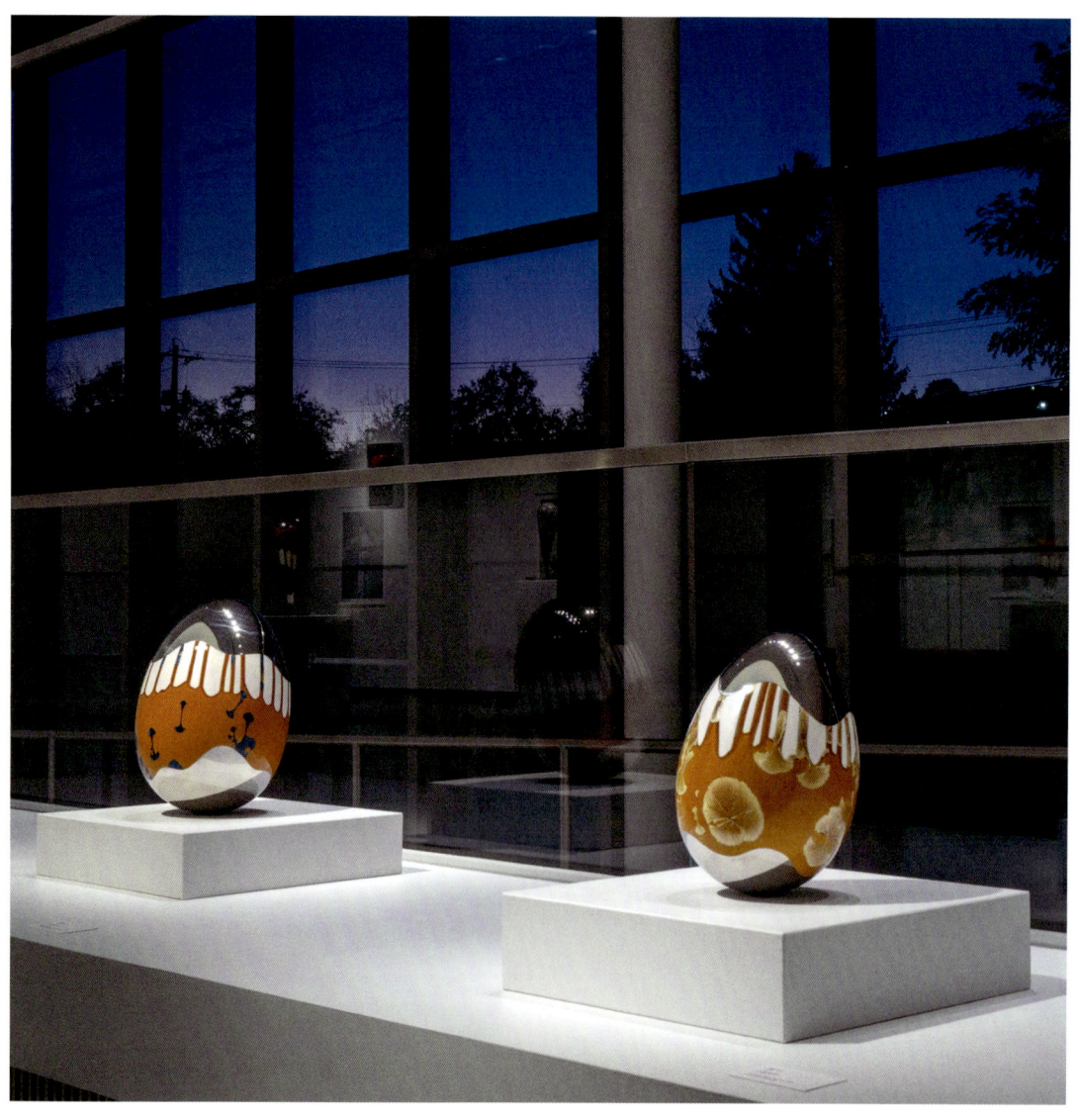

*Left: Li Hongwei,* Dan #11*, 2022, porcelain, stainless steel, 10.4 x 10.4 x 15.7 inches.*
*Right: Li Hongwei,* Dan #21*, 2024, porcelain, stainless steel, 8.7 x 8.7 x 13 inches.*

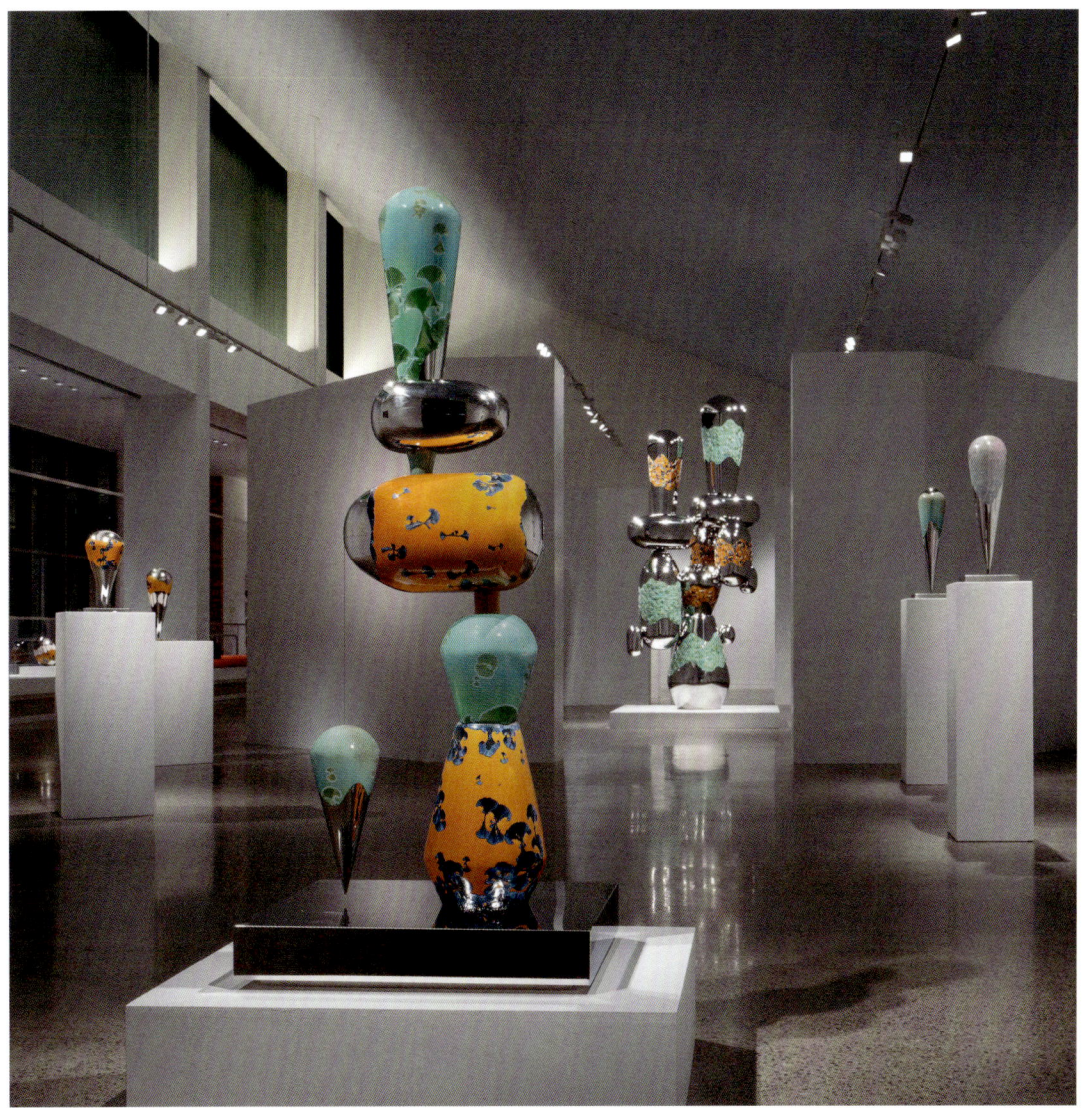

Constructing Radiance: Sculpture by Li Hongwei, *Gallery View, 2025*.

*Pages: 65-67:*
*Li Hongwei,* Beyond the Height #5,
*2024, porcelain, stainless steel,*
*60 x 43 x 138 inches.*

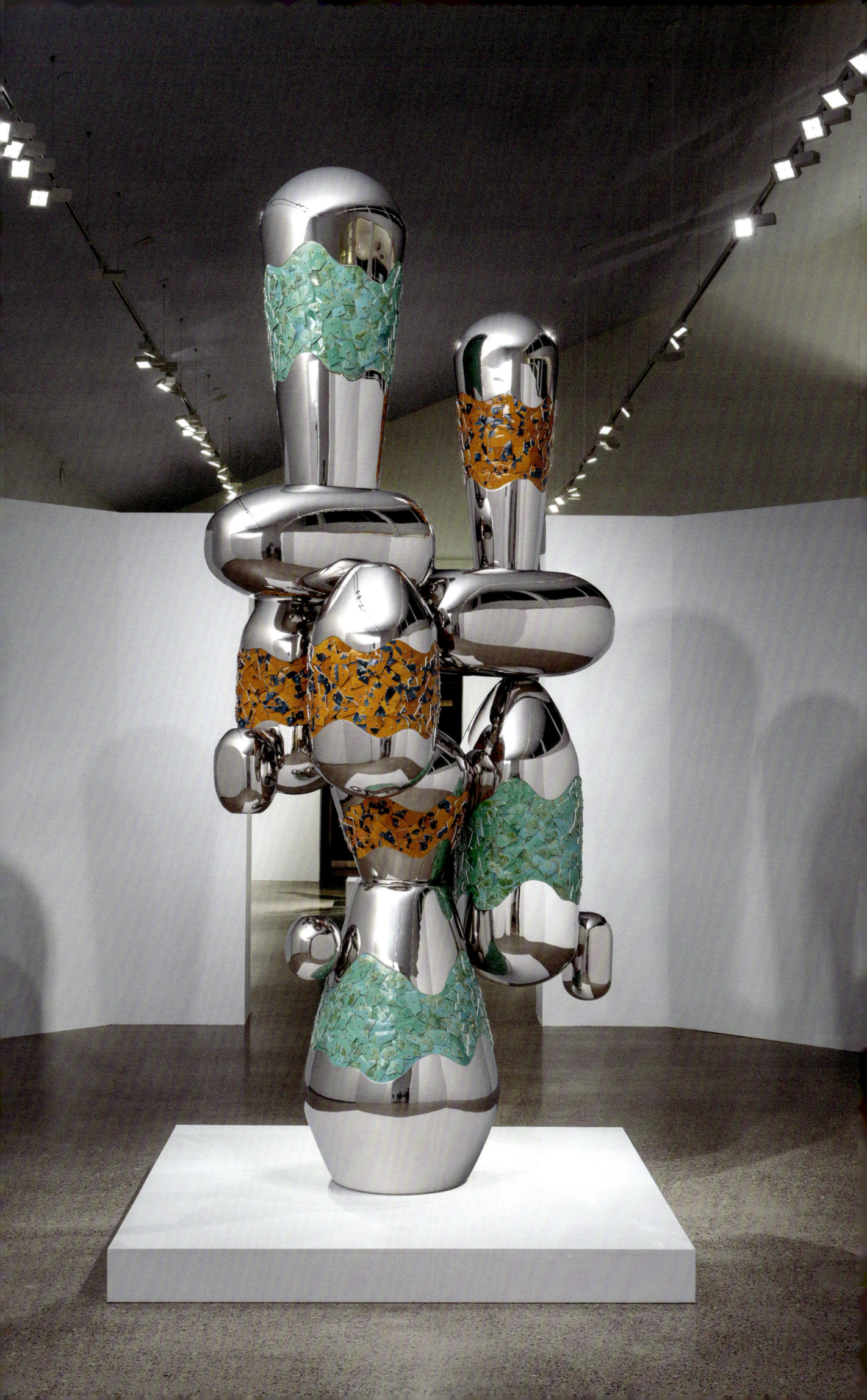

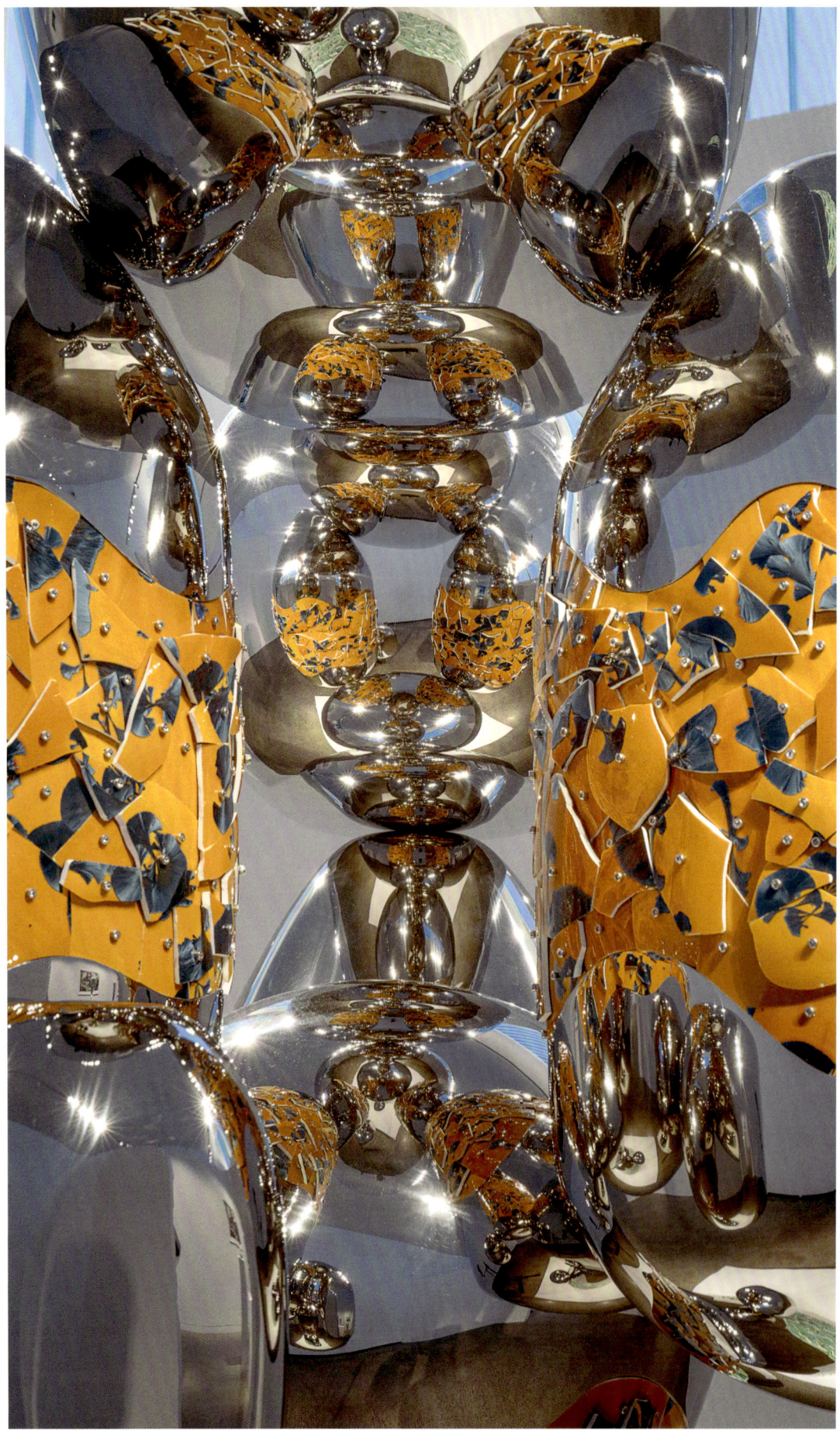

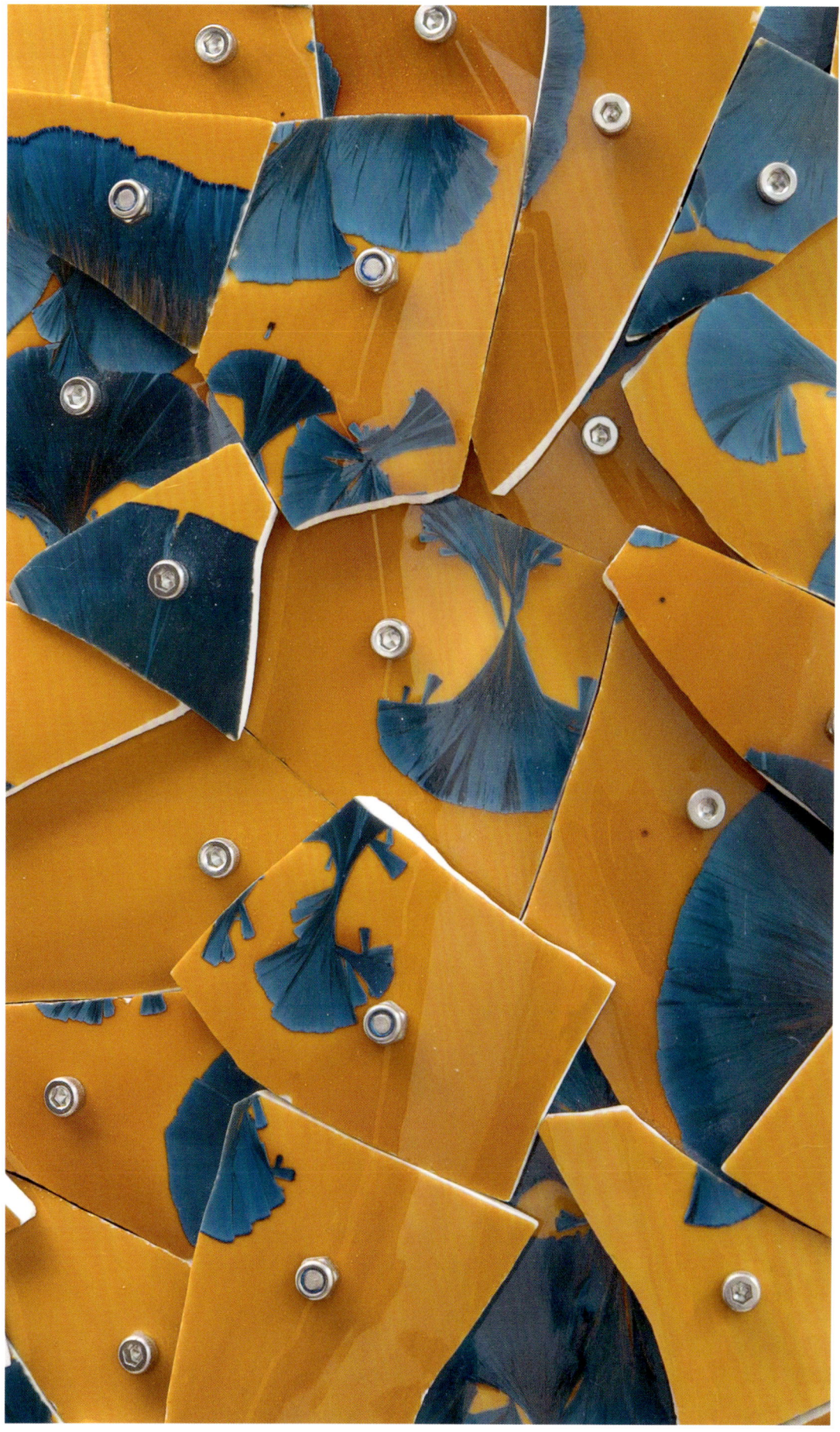

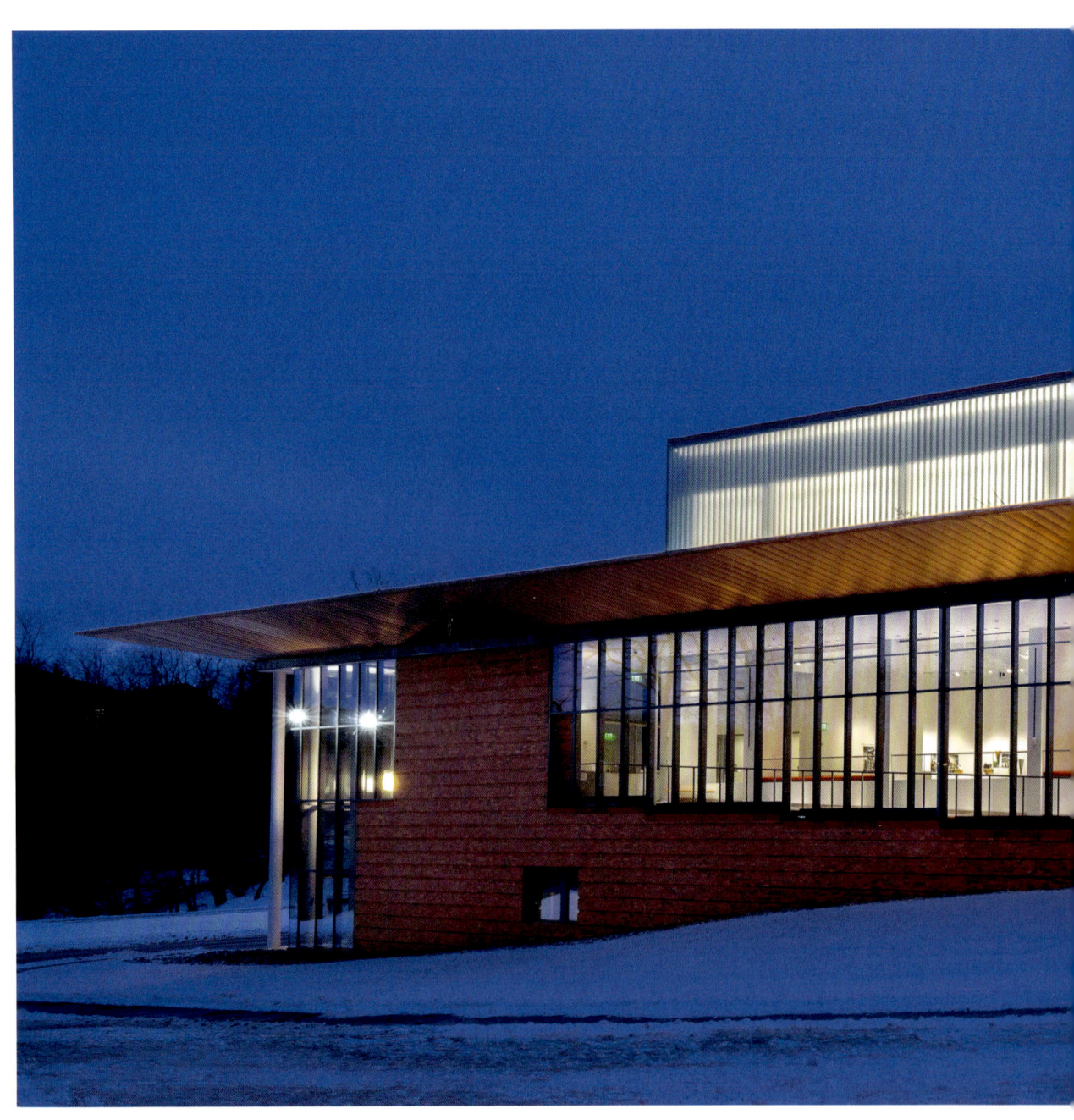

*Alfred Ceramic Art Museum, Winter Evening, 2025, Constructing Radiance: Sculpture by Li Hongwei.*

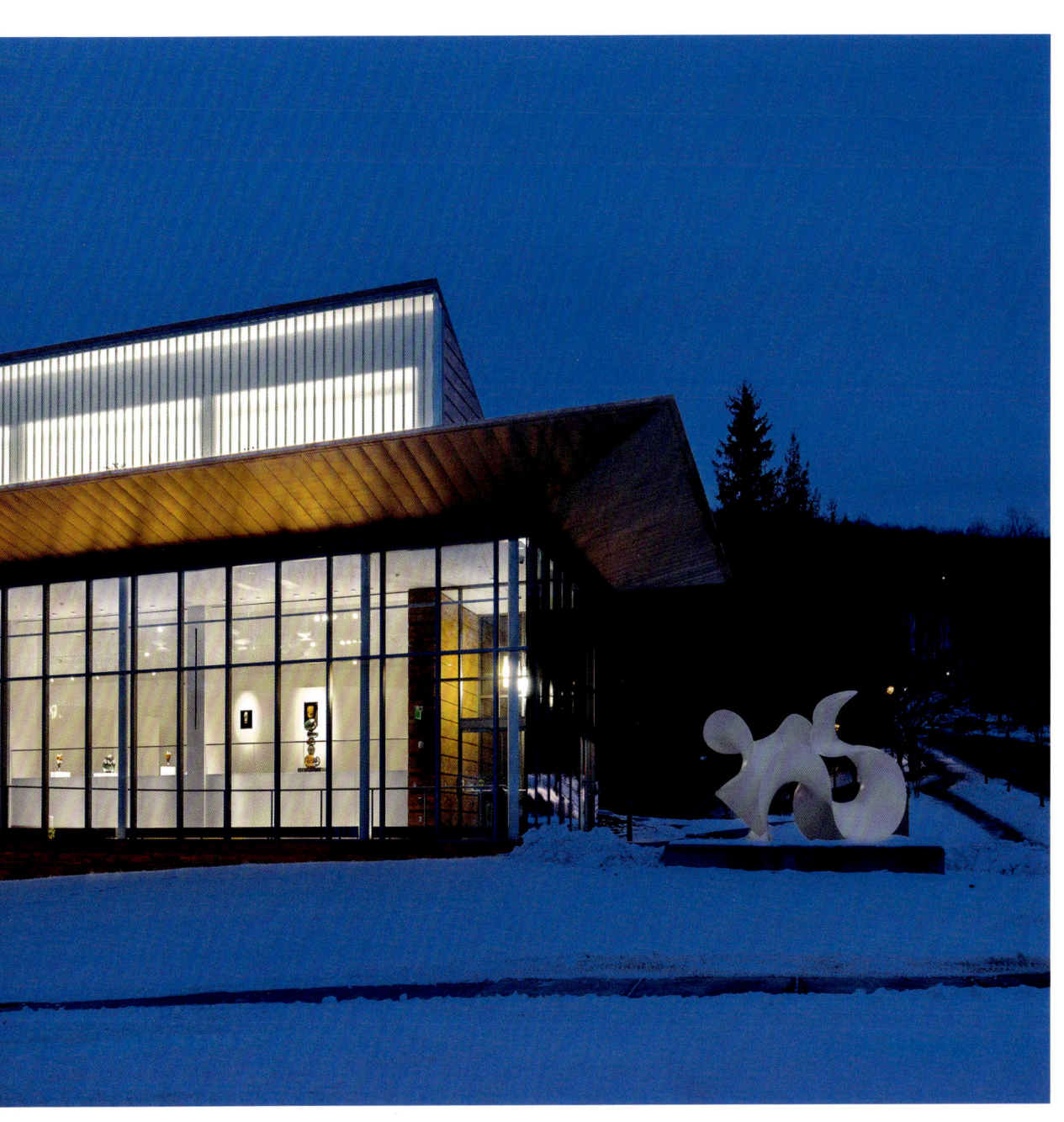

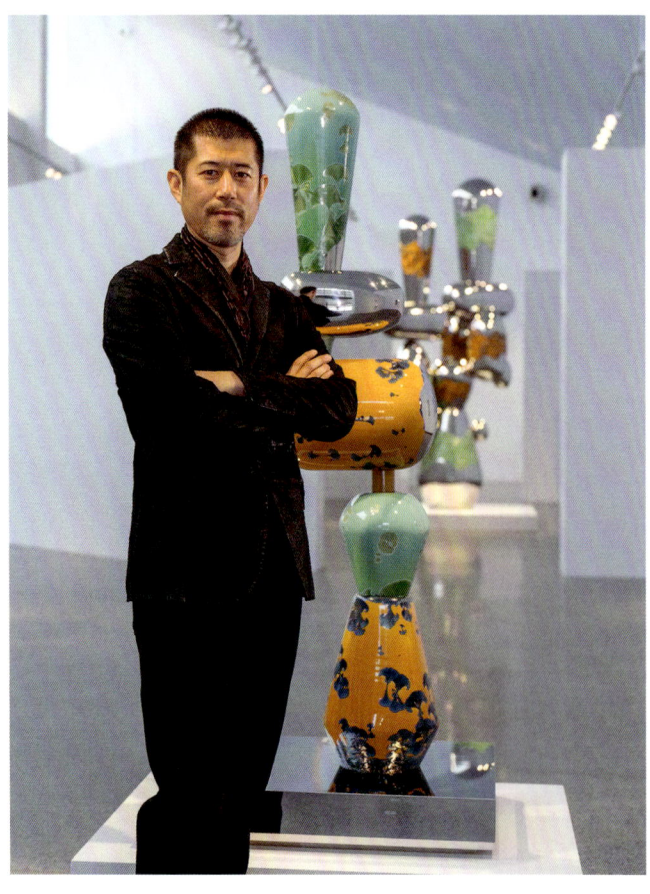

*Li Hongwei, 2025.*

# LI HONGWEI
# SELECTED RESUME

## Education

2007    MFA in Ceramic Art, New York State College of Ceramics at Alfred University, Alfred, NY

2005    BFA in Sculpture, Central Academy of Fine Arts, Beijing

## Selected Exhibitions

2026    Art in Public, Peabody Essex Museum of Art, Salem, MA (upcoming)

2025    Collection on view, Phoenix Art Museum, Phoenix, AZ

2024    Constructing Radiance: Sculpture by Li Hongwei, Alfred Ceramic Art Museum, Alfred, NY

2024    Master of Innovation: The Art of Li Hongwei, Pucker Gallery, Boston, MA

2024    Exterior Appearance and Inherent Quality: The Art of Li
        Hongwei, The Bay Gallery, Shenzhen, China

2023    Collection on view, Nelson-Atkins Museum of Art, Kansas City, MO

2022    Becoming Harmonious: The Art of Li Hongwei, Long Museum (West Bund), Shanghai

2022    Balancing the Cosmos: Works by Li Hongwei, Kalamazoo
        Institute of Arts, Kalamazoo, MI

2022    Brilliant Illusions: Crafted Forms by Li Hongwei, University
        of Kentucky Art Museum, Lexington, KT

2021   Collection on view, Philadelphia Museum of Art, Philadelphia, PA

2021   Sublime: Works by Li Hongwei, Pucker Gallery, Boston, MA

2019   Inner Reflection, Outward Transformation: The Art of
       Li Hongwei, Pucker Gallery, Boston, MA

2019   Collection on view, The Art Institute of Chicago, Chicago, IL

2019   New acquisition on view, Alfred Ceramic Art Museum, Alfred, NY

2019   US Embassy in Bishkek, Kyrgyzstan

2018   Exhibition of International Contemporary Ceramic Works,
       Tsinghua University Art Museum, Beijing

2018   Datong International Sculpture Biennale, Datong Museum of Fine Arts, China

2016   Core Sample, Collection on view, Alfred Ceramic Art Museum, Alfred, NY

2016   The Second National Exhibition of Contemporary Chinese
       Ceramic Art, National Art Museum of China, Beijing

2016   China – Ecuador Sculpture Exhibition, Quito, Ecuador

2015   Century Youth, 2015 China Russia International Fine Art
       Exhibition, Museum of The Imperial College, Beijing

2014   China The 12th National Fine Arts Exhibition, Taiyuan Museum of Fine Arts, Taiyuan

2014   Member Exhibition of International Academy of Ceramics, Dublin Castle, Dublin, Ireland

2013   Louvre Museum International Salon, Paris, France

2012   Member Exhibition of International Academy of Ceramics,
       New Mexico Museum of Art, Santa Fe, NM

2010   Scripps College 66th Ceramic Annual, Ruth Chandler Williamson Gallery, Claremont, CA

2008   Origins, Fox Art Gallery, University of Pennsylvania, Philadelphia, PA

## Selected Public Collections

The British Museum, London, UK

Museum of Fine Arts, Boston, MA

The Israel Museum, Jerusalem, Israel

Philadelphia Museum of Art, Philadelphia, PA

The Art Institute of Chicago, Chicago, IL

Harvard Art Museums, Cambridge, MA

Princeton University Art
Museum, Princeton, NJ

Yale University Art Gallery, New Haven, CT

Nelson-Atkins Museum of
Art, Kansas City, MO

Museum of Art, Rhode Island School
of Design, Providence, RI

Carnegie Museum of Art, Pittsburgh, PA

Bowdoin College Museum of
Art, Brunswick, ME

Phoenix Art Museum, Phoenix, AZ

New Orleans Museum of Art, New Orleans, LA

San Angelo Museum of Fine
Arts, San Angelo, TX

Everson Museum of Art, Syracuse, NY

Crocker Art Museum, Sacramento, CA

The Art Complex Museum, Duxbury, MA

University of Kentucky Art
Museum, Lexington, KY

Vassar College Art Museum,
Poughkeepsie, NY

Kalamazoo Institute of Arts, Kalamazoo, MI

Alfred Ceramic Art Museum, Alfred, NY

Herrick Memorial Library, Alfred
University, Alfred, NY

The Hun School, Princeton, NJ

Tang Teaching Museum, Saratoga Spring, NY

The Ashley Gibson Barnett
Museum of Art, Lakeland, FL

MGM COTAI, Macao, China

Mandarin Oriental Hotel Group, Beijing

China APEC International
Conference Center, Beijing

Long Museum, Shanghai

He Art Museum, Guangzhou

# WRITERS' BIOGRAPHIES

## WAYNE HIGBY

Wayne Higby is a Professor of Ceramic Art and the Wayne Higby Director and Principal Curator of the Alfred Ceramic Art Museum at Alfred University. His ceramic art works are held in the permanent collections of numerous art museums around the world including the Metropolitan Museum of Art, New York, the Smithsonian American Art Museum, Washington, DC, the National Art Museum of China, Beijing, the Hermitage Art Museum, St Petersburg, Russia, and the Museum of Modern Art, Tokyo. Higby's retrospective was held at the Smithsonian American Art Museum and documented in the book *Infinite Place: The Ceramic Art of Wayne Higby* published by Arnoldsche in 2013.

## DENISE PATRY LEIDY

Denise Patry Leidy currently serves as the Ruth and Bruce Dayton Curator of Asian Art at the Yale University Art Gallery. Prior to joining Yale, Dr. Leidy also served as the Brooke Russell Astor Curator of Chinese Art (emerita) at the Metropolitan Museum of Art, as well as in curatorial positions at The Asia Society New York, and the Museum of Fine Arts, Boston. She is endlessly fascinated by the development and movement of technologies, ideas, and images within and between Asian cultures, and between these centers and those in Africa, Europe and the Americas. In addition to curating exhibitions, she has published and lectured widely exploring topics in Buddhist art, Chinese and other Asian ceramics, and East Asian lacquer. Her publications include *Buddhist Art: Its History and Meaning, Mother-of-Pearl: A Tradition in Asian Lacquer, Wisdom Embodied: Chinese Buddhist and Daoist Sculpture in the Metropolitan Museum of Art, How to Read Chinese Ceramics,* and the recently released *Celadon on the Seas: Chinese Ceramics, 9th – 14th century.*

## BENJAMIN EVANS

Benjamin Evans is the Assistant Director and Curator of the Alfred Ceramic Art Museum. He has previously served as the director of two well-respected galleries, one in St. John's, Newfoundland and one in Brooklyn, New York. While living in Paris he launched his own curatorial project "Projective City," creating pop-up exhibitions in unused commercial spaces and a long-term collaborative project with Mixed Greens Gallery in New York City. Most recently Evans was the Communications Director at the International Academy of Ceramics, a member-driven organization in partnership with UNESCO whose goal is to foster international cooperation through a shared interest in ceramics. He holds five degrees, including an MFA from the University of Calgary and a PhD in Philosophy from the New School for Social Research.

*Li Hongwei, Allegory of Balance #40, 2024, porcelain, stainless steel, 26 x 18 x 50 inches.*